THIS IS HOW
SAVED PEOPLE

THE MEMOIRS OF A SAVED GIRL

Tisa Batey

ISBN 978-1-64515-458-7 (paperback)
ISBN 978-1-0980-0620-4 (hardcover)
ISBN 978-1-64515-459-4 (digital)

Christian Faith Publishing, Inc.
832 Park Avenue
Meadville, PA 16335
www.christianfaithpublishing.com

Printed in the United States of America

Contents

Acknowledgments

First, I want to thank God for giving me the insight and courage to write this book. In fact, were it not for the prompting of the Holy Spirit, I never would have considered writing this memoir. This was neither easy nor painless to write. It was, however, something I felt had to be done. The events of this book are loosely based on many of my life experiences that I've chosen to share with you.

Next I want to honor my parents Paul Jerry Batey (deceased) and Margie Douglass Moore for instilling in me the confidence to believe that I could accomplish anything. Because of you, I never experienced feelings of lack while growing up. You made sure my childhood was one filled with love and laughter. I am so blessed to have a mother who actually lived the life in front of us that she preached to us daily. I'm equally blessed to have had a father who loved his children more than life itself. One who was present in our lives and never ashamed to shower us with the affection children so desperately need. I will never forget the countless sacrifices you both made for your children. I'll never forget how often you must have gone without, only to ensure all our needs were met. We had a good life-a very good life…and I wouldn't trade it for anything in this world. God shined on us when He saw fit to bless us with two parents who loved us as much as you both did/do. I'll never forget!

Pastor Lionel Moore, we couldn't ask for a better stepfather. Not only are you a wonderful husband to our mother and a wonderful grandfather to our children but you also became one of my father's very closest friends while he lived. That's something very special and rare. You are the perfect example of a humble servant. Thank you for being just who you are. You're truly one of the most remarkable men I know.

I want to acknowledge my siblings Patrick (deceased) and Monique (Nikie) Batey for showing me unconditional love and support. Because of you two, I truly feel like I had the best childhood ever! I love the fact that even though we argued and had disagreements at times, we always had each other's backs. There is nothing we wouldn't do for each other. The love I have for the both of you is immeasurable and unwavering.

I absolutely *must* honor the most intelligent man I've ever known...the illustrious Bishop Dale C. Bronner for his incomparable spiritual guidance and leadership. I have learned so much both about God and myself since I joined Word of Faith Family Worship Cathedral in 2006. You made me look at Christianity in a completely different light. You helped me realize that following God can and *should* be fun instead of a chore! Anyone who really knows this man also knows that he has a heart after God. This resonates in how he leads his flock—not in arrogance or an attempt to usurp authority but in true love and compassion for his congregation. Myyyyy Bishop...I truly love you, man! In addition, I must thank his lovely wife, Dr. Nina Bronner. You have been a shining example of how a true woman of God should carry herself at all times. The love, adoration, support, and unparalleled respect you show to and for your husband has truly inspired me and many others to become the kind of wives any man would be proud to have.

Melanie Eskridge, we've been the best of friends since the sixth grade. Kelly Alicea, my luvbug, our friendship means the world to me. The bond I have with you two beautiful ladies has been unbreakable. Our friendship is easy...effortless. We just fit!

To my circle of friends, some old and some new...thank you for your unwavering love and support. I love you Shefon Harris, Ursula Relaford, Sharlene Bazel Parker, Dr. Ramona Coleman Bell, Soror Pam Rowe, Soror Tammi Smith, Soror Radiah Morman, Edward McSwine, Shatu Blake, Carlton Lampley, Darryl Harris and Cameron Taylor. My life has been so enriched as a result of your presence in it.

Lieutenant Colonel James Fearson, what can I possibly say about you? You are truly the most selfless man I have ever known. Your heart for others is pure, genuine, and uniquely made. I've turned to you for support when I've felt comfortable turning to no one else. And in true James Fearson fashion, you have been there for me—every time. I want you to know just how much I appreciate you for all you've done.

And last but certainly not the least, I want to thank my beautiful daughters Jazmen and Jhordyn Walker. Thank you for your unconditional love. Thank you for the respect you've always shown me. Thank you for allowing Mommy the freedom and time needed to write this book. Thank you for your belief in me. Love truly seems too weak a word to describe my heart for you. You two are my true inspiration—the wind beneath my wings—*my why*! I'm so thankful to God for allowing me the absolute pleasure of being your mom. I can only hope that I've made you both proud to call me your Mommy.

There are many more who have influenced me along this journey—too many to name. I have to believe you know who you are and the role you've played. Please know you all hold a very special place in my heart, and I thank God for you.

That Something

(For Tisa)

There's this something about me.
And when I enter a room,
The eyes, ALL of them,
In, on me, **ZOOM.**

There's something about me
That makes people Elevate!
**"Stand Tall, Be Positive,
We've no time for self-hate!"**

This something is overpowering,
Oozing from within,
Exuding intelligence and class,
While being your earthiest friend.

This something didn't stop me
From donning the masks,
While dealing with demons,
Lingering from generations past.

You would not believe what I have endured-
The humiliation, pain, the shame.
But I did it and hid it,
All in "Love's" name.

Years and years of masking,
Thinking I was happy,
Though I was not.
Trying to do it my way,
Instead of grasping the joy God's got.

Ignoring all the warnings,
Ignoring the red flags,
"Girl, he didn't mean it,
My words just made him mad!"

First we'd start off yelling,
Then he'd push and I might shove,
Before I even knew it,
He'd pull out the boxing gloves!

I couldn't believe it happened.
Twas like I was in a dream.
But then in romance after romance,
These scenes became routine.
But that SOMETHING about me,
Wouldn't allow me to stay....
There drenched in depression,
I knew I had to PRAY!

God used his Messenger,
On more than one occasion,
To inspire me to rise,
So with my life-
I stopped PLAYING!

"Depression is selfish"
Was he talking to ME?
Crying in the choir stand,
My pain was all I could see.

THAT SOMETHING SAVED ME,
Just like time upon time before,
Depression and self-pity,
Had to march out my door!

I shall **NOT** settle for anything less.
God's grace is sufficient,
And with His Mercy,
I am blessed.
That SOMETHING,
It protects me,
As it shines from deep within.
It's the light of my Savior,
And His LOVE
That never ends.

So, I shall not settle,
For what's just "good enough".
I'm not lowering my standards,
For in Jesus Christ I trust.

There **IS**
Something about Me,
Twas instilled from my **birth**.
Jesus Christ died for me,
So I know what I'm worth!

And I shall not settle....
Because...
There's **SOMETHING** about me!
-**Pamela Rowe** 2018

Chapter 1

The Beginning

I am not writing this book in an effort to *blow* the *whistle* on saved people. To the contrary, I am attempting to win souls into the kingdom of Christ. There is a huge misconception among those in the world that all saved people are *holier than thou*. I am here to dispel that myth. I am here to say that some of the most broken, sickly, and sinful people are the ones in the church. Many people living outside the will of God choose to remain there for fear of being judged or ridiculed by people who sin differently than they do. You see, the fact of the matter is that "we all sin and come short of the Glory of the Lord" (Romans 3:23). Nothing upsets me more than those who feel that, somehow, their sins are lesser ones than those of others. It's that sanctimonious and self-righteous attitude that prohibit us from doing that which we are commissioned to do as believers—winning souls to Christ. God sees all we do and knows all that we think. To Him, sin is sin. There are no big ones and little ones in His eyes. It's all sin, and they are equally offensive to Him.

If those in the world know that not all believers consider themselves perfect, then perhaps it will compel them to take the first step and simply enter through the doors of their local churches. It isn't God who nails us to the cross because of our sins but rather—*man*. Christ died for our sins. He died for the ungodly as well as the just. So if you are in the world, He died for you. He loves you and is waiting with open arms for you to come to Him. You just need to take that first step.

By writing this book, I hope I may be a catalyst that will propel you to do just that. I am not attempting to speak for all Christians. I am wise enough to know that there are those who will never come close to making some of the choices I've made; however, I also know that there are those who have done far worse, all while being in the church. I stand the risk of being judged, persecuted, ridiculed, and even ostracized over some of the poor choices I've made; however, that's a risk I'm willing to take if it means being obedient to the Holy Spirit. If I can help just one, then certainly, I have done a service with which God will be pleased.

My name is Tisa Batey-Walker, and my sins have been many! There is not one that I am proud of; however, I'm so glad that I serve a God who is just enough to forgive me for them all. I serve a God whose mercies are new each and every day. This means that every day, we are blessed enough to see, we have one more chance to get it right. It is of no concern to God what we may have done yesterday. He just wants us to repent, humble ourselves, seek His face, and turn from our wicked ways (Chronicles 7:14). He doesn't have a problem forgiving us. We have a problem forgiving ourselves—and others.

Although I have been ashamed of many things I've done, I am willing to unmask them if it means that just one soul will be won into the kingdom of Christ. I am allowing God to use me as a vessel in this war against the enemy. I am confident that when you read some of the sins I have committed, perhaps you won't be so hard on yourselves. Just maybe you'll realize that I am no better than you in God's eyes. And just *maybe*, you will realize that if God can forgive me, then certainly, He can and will forgive you.

Much of this book will be factual events which have occurred throughout my lifetime; however, some will be events that are loosely based on the realities that have occurred. In any event, the point still remains the same—We can overcome ourselves and any obstacles through Christ. He gives us the power to do all things if we just believe and trust in Him (Philippians 4:13).

I gave my heart to God at a very young age. I had a mother who had me in church several times a week and all day long on Sundays. I came from a religious family. Although they were some of the most loving people you would ever meet, their religious beliefs, often times, were at the center of much confusion, and it wasn't only my family. It was very common in the small town I came from. I did not learn the difference between religion and spirituality until I left home and started my own journey. And trust me when I say there certainly are major differences.

"Religion is the belief in someone else's experience. Spirituality is having your own experience" (Deepak Chopra). Being a religious person was important to my family when I was coming up. It was a status booster to them, and they wore it like a badge of honor. What I have since learned is that religion places you in a box, and spirituality frees you from that same box. Religion tells you what you should do while spirituality allows you to make your own decisions based on your own relationship and experiences with God.

"Religion causes division while spirituality seeks to unite. Religion is based on fear while spirituality is based on love" (Mindvalley Academy). The God I serve is a spiritual being; and since I was created in His image, I am spiritual—*not* religious. God cannot be contained in a box. He is much bigger than that. He is much too powerful to allow us to make Him what we want Him to be. He, alone, is God; and He does not need our help in assisting Him to be anything other than who He is.

I came from a family of very strong women. My mother and her sisters traveled the country singing the Gospel of Jesus Christ. They could do no wrong in my eyes. They were beautiful, talented, dominant, popular, and godly women. When they entered the room, everyone took notice. They were statuesque creations, and they never went unnoticed. I wanted to be just like them when I grew up. What I did not realize was that many of those traits would lead me to sin more than I could have ever cared to when I entered into adulthood. They possessed a strength that would often, although not intended, emasculate their husbands or significant others. Their need to have the last word and always be *right* often caused confusion. They made no apologies for the way they were, though. You could deal with them on their terms or not—the choice was yours. I was raised with this same mentality. That attitude was the cause of much confusion and dysfunction in my life, and it was not pleasing to God. "God is not the author of confusion but of peace and order" (Corinthians 14:33).

Growing up in my family meant never saying I'm sorry. It meant never admitting your wrongdoings but rather justifying them. It meant looking good on the outside but, at times, dying on the inside just to keep up appearances. It meant being way too prideful and arrogant at times because we were who we were. What I have come to realize, though, is that this was all sin in God's eyes. I'm not saying this to ridicule my family or to paint a negative picture that portrays them as bad people. To the contrary, they are truly some of the most amazing individuals I know. They have hearts of gold, and they truly love the Lord God. In fact, I have learned many wonderful and great things from them. They simply did what they knew to do. The harsh reality is that most influential families I grew up around in our small town were quite the same in many aspects. Perhaps it comes with the territory of being a part of a large and dominant clan.

I now know that the true measure of strength is being able to say I'm sorry and being able to walk away from conflict instead of engaging in it. This was a very hard life lesson for me and one that, at times, I still struggle with. The growth I have experienced through my faith does not make me perfect—just aware. When you know better, you do better. Or at least you should. When we enter into adulthood, it is up to us to either stay where we are or learn from our past experiences and grow. Were it not for the bad experiences in my life, I would not know the true character of God. I would not be able to testify of His goodness had I not been privy to some of the trials I've endured. So for that, I am grateful.

Not only were the women in my life strong minded; but if pushed, some of them could be provoked to violence. They didn't allow anyone to push them around or bully them in any way. They may not have started the conflict but trust me when I say they would certainly finish it. I'm convinced this was because of their upbringing. Their father, my grandfather, was from the Deep South. He was deeply rooted in the traditions of those of our ancestors. He was a stern man and a very strict disciplinarian, who was well respected not only in the community, but in his home as well. His reputation preceded him, in that he worked hard, minded his own business, and didn't welcome the opinions of others into his life or home. He was also known to be a pretty quick-tempered man at times, whose wrath; no one wanted any parts of. He married my grandmother when she was in her early teens, which was not uncommon back then. Together, they had eleven children—seven girls and four boys. In addition, he also fathered three outside children during their union.

My mother was the second oldest child and the eldest girl. That being said, much of her youth was spent raising her younger siblings. Commonly referred to as *Sis* by all her siblings, she was known to be the mean one! She didn't mess with anyone and didn't allow anyone to mess with her. Forced to grow up faster than any child should have had to, she married my dad at the tender age of only seventeen. Part of her reason for marrying so young was to get away from home. Don't get me wrong; she loved him, but had she been able to just be a kid herself, perhaps she would have waited a bit longer.

My mom always attributed Nanny, my father's mother, as being the one to teach her what real, unconditional love was. She never heard her parents tell her they loved her growing up, but she heard it from Nanny often. Not only did she tell her, but she showed her in every way. She showered my mother and us children with such an unconditional love. She left no room for anyone to question or doubt her love or commitment to her family. Although my mother knew and felt love from her parents, as children, it's also important to hear it.

She and my dad had a very good marriage in the beginning. They were deeply in love, and they made sure that we felt love from them. As I stop to reflect on our childhood, there are very few things I would care to change about it. Our lives were good and full of wonderful memories my parents afforded us. My mother was a very strict disciplinarian while my father was the exact opposite. We had the neighborhood house. Mom would not allow us to stay away from home much, but that was okay because there was always company at our house. Other parents felt completely comfortable allowing their children to come and stay with us. I remember taking family vacations every year, throwing annual Halloween parties, and probably one of the best memories was my mother and her sisters taking all us kids to Hot Wheels Skating Rink *every* Sunday night! That's right—they didn't send us. They took us. They all skated right alongside of us. Those were such fond memories—ones I will always cherish.

As time went on, unfortunately, things changed. As wonderful parents as they were to have and as much as they did to ensure all our needs were met, they eventually stopped meeting the needs of each other. At some point, those fun times became overshadowed by arguments and fights our parents would have. Although we did not witness the physical altercations between them, we knew of at least two of them. Both times, our father took a bullet from our mother. As I previously stated, she did not come for you; but she allowed no one to mess with her—*no one*!

The first time it happened, we were very young. I just remember my mother becoming infuriated over the fact that my dad had done something to her car to ensure she remained at home that day. In our minds, we thought she shot him just because he had messed with her ride. She was just mean! It would be more than 40 years later when I got up the courage to ask her about that day. The events that lead up to her pulling the trigger were quite different from anything I could have ever imagined.

My mother revealed to me that my father was seeing another woman…*a white woman*. Not only was he seeing her, but he had the audacity to allow her around our perfect little family from time to time. She would show up to the movies, ballparks and anywhere else we were together spending quality family time. She would ask to hold my baby sister and my mom would allow her to do so, oblivious to the fact that she was actually sleeping with my Daddy. I can only imagine how devastated and humiliated Mama must have been when her friends and family members revealed to her who this woman really was.

One night, after my mom learned of the affair, she followed my dad to see just where he was going. Her quest was unsuccessful, as my dad lost her in the pursuit. By the time she got back home my dad was already there. With a smirk on his face, he greeted her at the door with a very sly, "Where have you been?" She rolled her eyes and ignored his comments. The next day when my mom got in her car to go to work, it would not start. Her car would act up from time to time, so she lifted the hood to see what the problem was. What she discovered would infuriate her. My dad had cut all her wires under hood, obviously in an attempt to ensure she wouldn't be following him anymore. She was livid. He made sure she was stranded, not even considering the fact that she also needed her car for our benefit as well.

When my dad arrived home, I remember my mom telling her younger sister, who was there to babysit us, to just keep us outside and away from the house while she went in to confront my father. She said that an argument ensued about the car, and it eventually turned to the other woman. "If you want that bitch then go be with her." my mother said. This obviously infuriated my dad to the point of him slapping her with a force that was so hard it knocked her completely across the living room. Filled with rage he said "Don't you talk about her! Whatever you say about her, you say about me!" Wow! I couldn't believe what I was hearing. I couldn't believe my dad would do this to my mother. I always knew his love for her to be so incredibly strong and unwavering.

After she got herself up, she went to the bedroom to get her gun. She followed my dad in to the bathroom where he was getting himself together. "You've put your hands on the wrong one." she said before she pulled the trigger. After he was shot, he fell over into the tub; grabbing and pulling down everything he could get his hands on to aid in his fall. As he lay in the tub, my mother stood over him with the gun cocked and firmly pressed against his temple. She had every intention of killing him that day, but he began to beg and plead for his life. At that moment, she thought about her kids. She thought about how much we loved our father. And although not the best husband, she thought about how much he loved us and what a good father he was. She walked away from him without as much as a concern for him, gathered us up, and left him to fend for himself the best way he could.

We were quite young…I may have been 5 or so. I just remember being out in the yard, playing with my siblings as my aunt watched over us, when we heard that loud noise. "Oh my God, Sis done shot him!" my aunt yelled. We were so overtaken with all kinds of emotions. We all quickly ran into the house. I just remember seeing our father lying in the tub in the bathroom. He was still alive and I remember feeling so relieved. My mother walked away, very solemnly. She told us to get in our dad's car. As we were leaving, one of daddy's closest cousins was pulling up at our house. My mother, very coldly said to him, "You might wanna go in there and check on your cousin. I just shot him." She was as cold as ice and made no apologies for what she had done. We left and went to her parent's house for the evening just as though nothing at all had transpired.

We didn't know what to expect when we arrived back home. Was our mom going to go to jail? Was our dad in the hospital? Would our parents break up and never see each other again? I remember all these thoughts going through my head. Fortunately, the bullet just grazed my father. He was perfectly fine and intact when we arrived back home. He didn't even go the hospital, nor did he call the police to press charges against our mother. I remember feeling relieved…nervous, but relieved. What would come next? My mother never uttered another word about what happened to us, and we were always too scared to ask her about it.

The next time anything like this happened would be several years later. I was in my early teen years. They were actually divorced at the time and we had moved 2 or 3 times since that incident. My father had a really hard time letting my mother go after the divorce. He would stalk her and threaten anyone who tried to be with her. My mother went to the judge in our town, who happened to be a friend to her family. She reported my father for stalking her on a few separate occasions. She was finally able to secure a protective order and the cops would patrol our home from time to time to ensure she was safe. My father had such an unhealthy obsession for my mother. Even as kids, we could recognize it and it made us so very uncomfortable. He would interrogate us about our mother when he had us on the weekends. "Daddy, just stop asking us all these questions!" I remember telling him on several occasions. Although my father had a reputation for being a tough guy, he was quite the pushover when it came to his kids…especially my sister and me. We always felt so much love from him. We knew he would lay down his life for us in an instant if it came down to it.

This time, it was the middle of the night. I just remember waking up to hearing my mother say "I'm not taking any more licks from you!" Me and my baby sister, who shared a room together started screaming and hollering. My brother's room was on the other side of the house, but he eventually heard the commotion and joined us. By this time, my brother was older and becoming a young man. My brother loved our mother with all his heart and I truly feel that one reason he was given to her for such a short period of time, was to protect her…even if that meant from our own father at times. He had gotten to the point where he would stand up against Daddy when he and Mama were fighting "I'm not leaving, Daddy. I'm not scared of you anymore!" He always wanted to protect our mother…we all did.

This night, Daddy was destroying Mama's lingerie. "No other nigger will ever be able to see you in this." He was saying. I remember my mother coming into our bedroom, consoling us, "Everything is gonna be alright. I know you all are not used to seeing this anymore, but it's gonna be ok." As quickly as she came, she was gone. The argument ensued between her and my dad. And there it was again! That same sound we heard several years earlier. She had shot him again. I remember running out into the hallway that separated her bedroom from ours, only to see our father lying there shot…again. My brother immediately ran to my father in an attempt to pull him out of harm's way, as me and my sister ran to our mother. We were pleading with her to stop. "Mama, please don't kill our daddy. Please Mama…stops!" She had clicked by this time. Our cries were nothing more than mere distorted sounds to her. The hallway was dark. And it seemed much longer than it usually was. Mama was at one end of it and our father at the other. She pulled the trigger again…then again, but nothing. The gun was jammed. What we later came to realize was that when she was attempting to empty the rounds in to my father, my brother was still attempting to pull him out of harm's way.

Had the gun not jammed, my mother would have shot my brother directly in the back. In the midst of all this confusion, God was still present. My mother would have lost her mind had she the burden to carry of killing her only beloved baby boy.

I remember the police coming to our home, followed by my dad's mom and my mother's parents. She obviously knew the consequences of her actions and called them just in case she was arrested. My dad's mom grabbed my mother, crying and hugging her, "Margie, I love you so much." She said. Yes, my Nanny would side with Mama over her own son time and time again. She didn't uphold his wrong doings in any way. After that, my mother turned to the policeman, held her hands out in front of her and said "Do with me what you will." My mother was never arrested or charged with any crime or wrong doing. It was documented that she had repeatedly reported my father for stalking and harassing her. She was a federal government employee, and went on to retire from that same agency years later. Her reputation remained intact. She was still acknowledged and regarded as a strong pillar of strength in our community.

Years later, when I asked her why she never told us about this... the other women, all the physical and verbal abuse, she said "I didn't tell you because that was still your dad and I would never want to taint your image of him. Regardless of how he was as a husband, I knew how much he loved his children and how good he was as a father." I never knew the things my mom had to endure as a result of being with my dad...the public humiliation, the ridicule, the shame. We never knew.

As children, we were always hopeful that things would smooth out between them and that they would grow old together; but unfortunately, that just wasn't the case. In summary, they divorced and remarried a few years later only to ultimately divorce again for good when I was in college after twenty-four years of marriage. By this time, all I wanted was for them to be happy. And I can safely say that my brother, who was in the Navy, and my baby sister, who still resided with them at home, felt the same way. The separation wasn't at all painful for us the second time. As a matter of fact, we welcomed it.

Chapter 2

The Marriage

"Tisa, you can't do this. What makes you think you could ever own a successful business? How many times have you tried and given up? That's just what you do. You are meant to do exactly what you are doing right now for the rest of your life! And don't even think about getting married again…or even having a stable relationship. You know good and well, you don't do those. The man you want does not exist! You know you're way too picky for what you bring to the table. Your family is socially dysfunctional, and so are you."

These are the thoughts that consumed me both day and night. No matter how hard I tried to convince myself, otherwise, I didn't seem to be able to gain control over my thoughts anymore. And those very same thoughts began to sabotage everything in my life—from business ventures to personal and professional relationships. I just wanted to give up. It was just too hard. I refused to stop beating myself up for mistakes or poor decisions I had made over my adult years.

I wanted desperately to be that woman who made her mark in this life—the woman who left a legacy for her children to be proud of. I wanted to make a difference; however, all I seemed to be doing was destroying everything that came across my path. And I was doing this with my thoughts. Where did this person come from? When did I become this negative-thinking woman? Why? I was the one who had it all, literally—a good career, solid marriage, beautiful kids, home of my dreams, and a strong faith in God. Where did it all go? And more importantly, how did I go about getting it back? I realized that a trail of bad relationships and bad decisions had really destroyed the confidence I once had in myself. I came to feel as though I had let God down so many times that He was just punishing me for all the wrongs I had done.

I met whom I thought was my *soul mate* twenty-five years ago. I had just graduated college and moved from a very small town in East Tennessee to the happening city of Atlanta, Georgia. He was the most beautiful man I had ever laid my eyes on. My close girlfriend had come in from Tennessee to visit me for the weekend, so I took her and another local friend out for the evening to a popular sports bar. As cliché as it may sound, I truly did spot him from across a very crowded room. I saw him when he entered the bar and told my girl-friends that I absolutely *had* to meet this man. It was, literally, love at first sight for me. Unbeknownst to me, as I was building up the courage to approach him, my homegirl, who had earlier left our table and her date to go to the restroom, was beating me to the punch. My heart sank when she told me that she had just met him and given him *her* number. I was pissed! I wanted to slap the hell out of her! I wanted to stomp her ass in the ground!

How could she do this to me? I thought. I just told her how much I wanted to meet this guy. Who does that? Isn't that a direct violation of every girl code in the book? So what did I do? I'm so very glad you asked that question. I smiled and pretended to be happy for her. I took the high road by convincing myself that I had no right to be upset. I mean, I had never actually met the guy. He was fair game, and she got to him first.

Over the course of the next few months, I started dating some-one else. He was part of a popular R & B duo back in the early '90s. I attended one of their concerts with my best friend and her family from Tennessee who stopped in Atlanta and picked me up for a road trip to Tuskegee, Alabama. He saw me from the stage and had someone in his entourage come and escort me backstage when the concert was over. Our relationship became pretty serious in a relatively short period of time. But that wasn't unusual for me. I had become accustomed to getting what I wanted when I wanted it to some degree. At that time, he did it for me, and I wanted him. I had always been a bit of an over achiever who viewed very few things as a real challenge. Things came easily for me back then—because that's what I expected. I had full control over my thoughts. And they were both positive and powerful! I imagine it was because of the strong Christian values instilled in me from a young child. I was always taught to ask for what I wanted and then expect to receive it. That's pretty much how I governed myself throughout my life.

I would, however, see Calvin, the soul mate, over the next several months more than I would have liked or was even comfortable with. Each time I would go home to Tennessee, my girlfriend would always ask if he could ride in with me to see her. In addition, each time she would come to town, we would all hang out. We became very cordial with one another; and although I was still attracted to him, I was not the kind of chick that would ever allow myself to get caught up with anyone a friend had dated. Besides, my focus was elsewhere. I was now committed to someone else. He was fascinating to me, and I enjoyed a few of the perks that came along with dating a celebrity. I was content and completely faithful to him despite the fact that his demons were trying to convince him otherwise—and winning.

He was extremely jealous and insecure. Not to mention consumed with his own guilt over how he was obviously conducting himself on the road. I never had a problem trusting him because I felt so much love from him. We were both very young, though; and he seemed easily influenced by other members of the band. They would tell him how stupid he was for trying to be faithful when the groupies were so easily accessible and willingly accommodating. Although to this day he has never admitted to it, I believe he would eventually succumb to all the peer pressure. And I believe his feelings of guilt materialized through his accusations toward me. He would tell me that he was scared of getting hurt. He always felt as though he needed to guard himself against me to a certain degree. I began to grow really tired of the senseless arguments and the need to feel as though I had to defend myself when I knew I was doing nothing wrong. I was too young to realize that he was actually telling on himself through it all.

We called it quits on this one particular Friday morning. I was heading in to Tennessee later that day, and Calvin was riding in with me to see my friend. He could sense that I was a little sad, and I began to confide in him about what had transpired earlier that day. I later discovered that although he was attempting to console me with encouraging words, he was actually elated on the inside that things hadn't worked out. Little did I know that he was as drawn to me from the beginning as I had been to him.

He would throw little subtle hints over the next few weeks that would leave me wondering. For instance, he would call me, out of the blue, to check up on me after the break up. He would ask me to go with him to work out. He would come pick me up and show me around Atlanta to help me become more acclimated to my new home. He would come to my apartment complex to play beach volleyball with me after work—and he knew absolutely nothing about volleyball. I was delighted to teach him as I played the sport in college and actually received all conference honors.

Encounters like these continued for a period of time until he finally made his move. He called me one day while I was at work and told me that he had been thinking of me and that he was missing me. He asked if he could come by later that day to talk to me. I knew then that my suspicions were valid. He wanted me just as I did him. I had a ton of mixed emotions over how my girlfriend would feel. However, my attraction to him was magnetic, and it overshadowed any feelings of guilt I may have had. We became inseparable from that point on. I began to push back from communicating with my girlfriend as much…out of discomfort—not guilt. I never felt guilty because the relationship felt so right.

My phone rang one morning when Cal and I were in bed. "Tisa, hey chick! What's up?" It was her. "Hey girl…not much." I replied. She continued, "Hey, I need to ask you something and I need you to be honest with me." Silence followed, as I knew exactly what she was preparing to ask me. "Are you and Calvin seeing each other?" She asked. "Yes we are." I replied, without even a thought. Although she was hurt, she acknowledged that she knew something like this might eventually happen. Fortunately, we were able to move past this uncomfortable situation and rebuild our friendship to beyond what it even was prior to this debacle.

Although Calvin and I spent all our free time together, there were things about him that he did not reveal to me initially—things about his lifestyle. He convinced me that he was a businessman. He told me about all these great investments he had made with monies he acquired from a lawsuit involving a motorcycle accident he had. I was so enamored with this man. He had it all—looks, intellect, money, and he was pleasing in bed. I had it all once again! I had never been happier—ever! What I would soon discover was that I was dating a drug dealer. By that time, though, I was already deeply in love with him as he was with me. He was very strategic in how he won me over, but he did just that—won me over. I had grown very comfortable with the lifestyle I was afforded, so I never encouraged him to stop. In a very short period of time, I had fallen head over heels in love with this man. I just didn't want my parents to ever find out what he really did. I was so incredibly naïve to think that they never would.

He was good to me, and I enjoyed being spoiled by him. I was only twenty-three years old, and I had no idea just how dangerous this lifestyle could be. All I knew was that I was with the love of my life, and we were having a ball. I never even allowed myself to imagine that anything bad could ever happen. I remember what my dream car was back then. It was the Honda Accord. He helped me purchase one from a friend who had one he was selling. It was practically brand-new and top-of-the-line. I was on cloud nine. To top it off, he took me home to Detroit to meet his parents. Little did I know he was also planning on proposing to me while we were there. We went ring shopping with his mother, and he purchased me a beautiful engagement ring. We had only been dating for three months, but it seemed as though we'd known each other forever.

This was also the first time I saw the *other* side of Calvin. He was always high strung but relatively mild-tempered. We had an argument shortly after checking into the hotel we were to stay in. I had always been quite the mouthy one when trying to convey my point, and I had always owned that. It came naturally for me, and I never had a reason to want to change it. Calvin hit me on my jaw as a result of our argument which was over him communicating with another chick. My jawbone immediately did its own thing. Of course, he was extremely apologetic, and I was extremely forgiving. Although I had never been in a physically abusive relationship, I was no stranger to it. I came from a family of very violent relatives—grandfather, uncles, aunts, and even my parents.

He was very apologetic and I loved him so much until it wasn't even a choice as to whether or not I would forgive him. The unfortunate thing was that I had to meet his family for the very first time, with a swollen jaw. I'm sure his parents questioned him about it at some point while we were there; however, the entire family acted as though they didn't even see it in my presence. It was simply never spoken of.

I was excited to show my ring and car off to all my friends when I returned. I truly felt like we had it all—but it would be short-lived. One night, when we were going out, Calvin noticed a man sitting in his car, watching our every move. I remember feeling a little concerned. I asked him if he thought everything was going to be okay, and he assured me it would be. That was all I needed to hear to feel better. I thought nothing more of it. I felt very safe and secure with Calvin. He soon became my everything. I loved him more than I had ever loved anyone. You see, the trust I should have placed only in God, I put it in man. This would prove to be a grave mistake. And one I would pay for later on in life.

I remember my father coming to visit us shortly after we returned from Detroit. My jaw was still bruised; however, most of the swelling had gone down. My dad immediately noticed it and began to question me about it. Calvin was right there, but even if he had not been, I still would have never revealed the truth to my dad. He was a real hothead over his children, and I feared what he may have done to Calvin at that time. I could tell Cal was nervous by his line of questioning—very nervous. I told my dad I hit it up against something. He obviously did not believe me. He grabbed my face and started to look at it very closely—turning my chin from side to side. I could see Calvin out of my peripheral vision, and he was watching my dad like a hawk. My dad made one comment and never revisited it. He said, "You've always been such a beautiful young woman, and I would hate to think about what I would do to anyone who ever tried to change that!" Although he was talking to me, he was indirectly speaking to Calvin. He needed Calvin to hear him loudly and clearly—and he did!

My lease was up on my apartment, and we decided we would move in together. We chose a larger two-bedroom apartment a few miles up the street. Shortly thereafter, life as we knew it would change forever. One weekend, we had company in town from Detroit—Calvin's older brother and a couple of his friends. Cal left out early Saturday morning to meet a *client*. He said he would be back within the hour. I began to get myself ready for the day we had planned together. We would take in a little shopping, a movie, and dinner. Several hours passed, and he still wasn't back nor was he answering his phone. I was starting to get worried when someone knocked on our door. It was a female asking for him. I definitely needed to know who this was, so I opened the door. As soon as I did, we were bombarded by police seemingly coming from every direction. They had already arrested Calvin, and now they came to search our residence. Although I had no dealings with drugs or any of his transactions, I was also apprehended because the drugs were found in our apartment and both our names were on the lease. I can remember lying, handcuffed, on the floor along with my brother-in-law and two others who were there visiting, while they searched our apartment. All I could think about was how Calvin was doing. I wondered if they hurt him. I laid there facing the biggest debacle of my life, and my only concern was for the man I loved.

My father called us that Saturday as he did almost every day, and he could not reach us. Calvin's brother, who was still at our place, continued to make up reasons why we were not available to talk each time he called. My dad began to worry. He could feel that something was wrong; however, Jay was relentless and refused to tell my father that we were in jail. I got out around noon on that Monday after having spent two days in jail. I refused to eat or drink anything while I was there, so I quickly dropped 10 lb. The other ladies there were only happy enough to divvy out every meal I received among themselves. They treated me as if I were a Barbie doll. They would talk about me as if I weren't even in the room. I can remember two of the girls getting into an argument about me. The first girl thought that I should break things off with Calvin because he exposed me to this mess I was in. The second chick thought I should stick it out with him. She could tell he took good care of me by looking at my hair and nails. She thought it was apparent that he spoiled me. They were rough around the edges and certainly not unfamiliar with the inside of a jail cell. They were cool, though. They became protective of me, and I felt covered. They would tell me how obvious it was that I didn't belong there. When they finally called my name over the intercom to release me, they all started to applaud. They seemed genuinely happy for the fact that I was getting out. Although I never saw them again and probably wouldn't recognize them if I did, there was a bond formed—a bond of sisterhood.

As soon as I was released, I called my father. I knew he was extremely worried, and it would be only a matter of time before he showed up on our front porch if he didn't hear from me. I could tell he was relieved but still worried. I assured him that everything was okay by telling him Calvin and I had just gone out of town for the weekend. I don't think he believed me, but he stopped asking questions. He was just relieved to hear his baby's voice. He was good with just knowing I was alright…at least for the moment.

Calvin had insisted that I be bonded out first, so he remained incarcerated while we worked to come up with the money to get him out. His bond was much more costly than mine. Between his parents and a partner he ran drugs with, we were able to bond him out within a week or so. The cops had confiscated the safe we had in our apartment, along with all the thousands of dollars located inside it. I was so happy to have him home. I was so excited until I forgot to call his parents to let them know. His mother, who had treated me coldly from the day I met her, was not at all pleased. I apologized for not reaching out to them prior to her calling me. Her response floored me. "Ain't this a Bitch? Y'all were ringing the phone off the hook while you were trying to get him out." I later grew to know that was just how she was at that time...very direct, cold, and even hurtful.

I became pregnant shortly after all this happened. It was no accident as Cal had asked me to stop taking birth control. Part of me wondered if this was his way of ensuring I'd be here when and if he had to do time. I knew he was the man I wanted to spend my life with, so it didn't matter to me at all. We made a visit to the justice of the peace on a random weekday evening and got married. I was almost seven months pregnant, and it was just the two of us.

All the charges against me were dropped because Cal took responsibility for all the drugs found in our apartment; however, his court date was quickly approaching. Calvin was convicted and spent the first three and a half years of our marriage in prison. Our first child was only one month old when her father went away. I did my part to ensure our marriage remained solid, and our child knew her father. I moved back to Tennessee at the urging of my parents. They knew I would benefit from having a strong support system in place as I knew nothing about being a mother. They helped me through a very rough period in my life, and I will be forever grateful to them.

Although I lived in Tennessee, I was on the road every weekend to visit my husband in Gainesville, Georgia. Most weekends, I would bring the baby, so she could bond with her dad. It was extremely important to me that she knew who her father was. Initially, I was a basket case. I truly didn't know how I was going to survive without him for three years. We had never spent any time apart, and I was so accustomed to the comfort I felt going home to him every day. I remember having a conversation with my mom. "Mama, I don't know what I'm gonna do without Calvin. I just can't handle all this pain I'm feeling right now."

She asked me only one question. "Do you truly love this man... truly?" I told her I certainly did and her reply was very short and direct. "Then you need to stick by him." After putting our baby to bed, I would cry myself to sleep every night. The emotional pain was unbearable at times. I learned to lean and depend on God again, and things eventually got easier for me. I had drifted pretty far away from

Him since I had been with Calvin. He didn't know God, and I did a poor job of introducing the two of them. Cal had plenty of time to become acquainted with Him now, and that's exactly what he did. He grew closer to God and formed his own personal relationship with Him. I began to see a positive change in him more and more each day as he learned to lean on God to see him through his current situation.

There were many attacks on our marriage, and they were compounded with the fact that we were apart from one another. Although Cal was in a minimum-security camp, conjugal visits were not permitted. This was extremely difficult for him since he was a young man in the prime of his life. He formed a close relationship with one of the officers there, and we were permitted to be together on numerous occasions. It was not at all fulfilling to me as the locations and surroundings were not always ideal. But I knew it was what he needed, and I chose to avail myself whenever I could. What came next was a complete shock to the both of us.

I became pregnant as a result of one of our encounters and was totally devastated. I didn't know what to do—for numerous reasons. What would people think of me becoming pregnant while my husband was away? What would the backlash be from my current employer? I was a news anchor, and that would not set well with them since it was all about appearances. What would the church folk think of me? Would they think I cheated on my husband? What would happen to Calvin when I began to show and his opposing officers discovered we had been together sexually? What consequences would he have to endure? How in the world would I support another mouth to feed? There were so many thoughts that consumed me on a daily basis. Cal and I made the toughest decision we would ever make. We decided to terminate the pregnancy. We made this decision alone and without anyone else's knowledge or input. I did what I felt I had to do at the time; and although we never discussed it again, the guilt would follow me for the rest of my days. God could never forgive me for this one. There's no way! So I pushed this so far back in my mind until I have to focus on it to remember it now. I listened to and believed the pro-choice people whose mission was to convince us that the fetus was not yet a real baby. That gave me comfort, and I held on to that tightly.

I moved back to Atlanta later that year and began working for the nation's largest rent-to-own company. They were recruiting college graduates for their fast-track management program, and I just needed to secure a job that would afford me the ability to relocate back to Atlanta. It was a moderately lucrative venture for me at that time and paid much more than my anchoring position at a very small station back in Tennessee. I learned a lot about business management and excelled very quickly within the company, eventually running the largest sales volume store in all of Georgia. My supervisor became very smitten with me after being there for a while, and we became personal friends as a result. He was a white man who was married to a sister. They had one child, and she was the same age as our little girl. He took me under his wing and taught me everything he knew about the business and management. He was very tall, athletic, handsome, and intelligent. The way he interacted with customers, toppled with his obvious confidence, was very appealing to me. And we became quite close over the two-year period we worked together.

Although I remained physically faithful to Calvin, emotionally, I was not committed. I knew that my boss had developed genuine feelings of love for me, and I enjoyed our friendship. He became my shoulder—my confidant—and I looked forward to seeing him each day. I knew he would be good to and for me; however, I knew that leaving Cal was not an option, so I resisted. It was difficult, but he respected my decision to stay by my husband's side—and that's just what I did. He and his wife ended up divorcing, and I always felt as though I had something to do with it. I knew his heart was with me, and he did not attempt to hide that fact. I felt really bad because I knew I couldn't be what he needed or wanted me to be. Although we remained in contact until Cal came home, he received a promotion; so we no longer saw each other on a daily basis. This made things a bit easier for him to handle. We would eventually lose all contact with one another.

The toughest hurdle for our marriage, though, came in 1997 when I lost my only brother in a car accident. His death hit me like a ton of bricks, literally. The pain was more than I felt I could bear. I felt like I wanted to die. I saw no light at the end of this dark tunnel. My insides ached, and any romantic feelings I had for Calvin dissipated. The only feelings that consumed me were total and complete sadness and devastation. My brother was a tower of strength in my life, and his death was unfathomable to me. Shortly after his death, I went to see Cal in prison. He was talking about my brother and how much he loved him and would miss him. I completely lost it and broke down crying. In the midst of my tears, Calvin made the most insensitive comments I had heard from anyone since my brother's death had taken place.

"Tee, I know your brother is gone, but it should give you some comfort to know that you still have me here. Doesn't that make it easier for you to handle?"

I absolutely could not believe what I was hearing. Although I knew he was only attempting to comfort me, it angered me to know he had the capacity to be so selfish. He did not like to see me cry, so I began to hide my grief from him. I realized that I had to be strong rather I felt like it or not. I convinced myself that my brother was still in the Navy and was stationed in Japan, as he was several years prior to his death. I told myself he would return home soon and that I would see him again one day. I pushed his death so far back in my mind until it was no longer a reality to me. This would prove to be a grave mistake for me. One I would live to regret.

Calvin was released the next year, and I was able to bring him to the home I had attempted to create for the three of us. Things felt very awkward for me. My feelings for him, admittedly, had changed; however, I vowed to never let him know this. It would already be difficult enough for him to become acclimated back into society without me putting this burden on him. So I put my big-girl panties on and prepared myself for a life with my husband. I knew then that I no longer needed him. I knew that I could make it without him if I so chose to do so. I had grown comfortable being without him, and I could not help feeling this way. I didn't want or choose these feelings, but they were there. My heart had really hardened since my brother's death. I was not grieving the way I needed to. I didn't feel I was afforded to support to do so. There was a huge piece of me that was just gone. And I had no idea how to get it back—or if I ever even would.

Calvin seemed somewhat bitter toward me, though. I think it was because I had freedom while he was locked up. It didn't seem to matter that I was visiting him almost every weekend of his incarceration or that I had given up just about all extracurricular activities so that I could be with him. He just seemed bitter. One thing he said to me stuck out like a sore thumb. "Tisa, you chose to stay with me." I didn't ask you to, so I don't feel like I owe you anything." He made it clear that it was my choice, not his. This was hard to hear or take. And although I didn't like it, I took it. There was a part of me that felt guilty because of the emotional relationship I had developed with my boss. A part of me felt like he knew—like he could just sense it. I never shared it with him, though. I just didn't feel like he would be able to handle it. So that became something else I would just tuck away in my memory bank.

We went on to achieve some really great things together. Financially, God had blessed us. We both had good jobs, and we were able to purchase our first home a year after he was released. We had a beautiful home, nice cars, and had joined a new church family. Things really seemed to be going great for us; however, I felt somewhat empty inside. Make no mistake, I truly loved my husband; however, there were certain things I longed to feel with my husband that I just no longer felt. He was very easily distracted by other women—always had been. He would allow himself to get caught up in the compliments and conversations they offered him. He would say it was because I was not affectionate enough after I became a mother. He always bragged to me and others about how I was the only woman he had *never* cheated on—in his life. He was very proud of this fact and wore it like a badge of honor. I knew my husband loved me as he had never loved another woman; however, one thing I was certain of was that when he stopped bragging about it, it stopped being the reality. Why did I not pray for God to restore the love I once felt for him? I ask myself that question over and over. I can't answer it. I prayed for many things but never that.

I can remember one day I had been in my closet crying over my brother. I missed him so badly, but I felt I had to hide my grief as not to disappoint or worry Calvin. I pretended like I was all better, but nothing could have been further from the truth. He noticed I had been crying when he saw me. He hugged me and would always attempt to comfort me; however, I knew it worried him. A few days later, we were arguing about something. He began to talk about how much I had changed since my brother passed, and then he said the *unthinkable*. "Tisa, you should've just married your brother instead of me." This was, without a doubt, the most damaging thing he had ever said to me. It hurt me to my core. And although I was a private person, too private at times, I shared this comment with my family. That one comment changed the entire dynamics of not only my relationship with him but also his relationship with the rest of my immediate family. My dad, who Cal spoke with daily, stopped calling him. My mom was just outdone. Her opinion of him had changed drastically; and for that period of time, she wanted nothing to do with him. And my baby sister, well, let's just say, he was dead to her.

It was probably a few months that passed before things would eventually return to normal. Cal apologized to both me and my family. I still held on to feelings of resentment, though. Each time he would hurt me, I would allow my heart to harden more and more. I was good at saying "I forgive you," but I seldom let things go. It became very easy for me to go to church several times a week, sing in the choir on Sunday mornings, give God praise with all I had within me, and then come home and not speak to my husband for a week at a time. I had mastered the art of being a hypocrite. And that's hard for me to say, but it's the harsh reality. I was more concerned with the outward appearance of our marriage than I was with praying to God and allowing Him to restore it.

We had our second child three years after he returned home. It took him and our first daughter months of pleading with me to try and have another child before I finally gave in. I was content with just the one. Besides I knew there were problems within our marriage, and I wasn't convinced that having another child was the right decision. Divorce was never an option for Calvin, though, so he was certain we needed to try to have another child. I gave in, and we had another beautiful baby girl. She brought so much joy into our lives. I was so proud of how well he took care of her. He would do as much, if not more with and for her, as I did. He was really a good father not only to the baby but to both our girls. He was always the one who captured every moment of our lives on film or camera. He was always snapping pictures or videoing events of our lives. For a period of time after her birth, things really seemed to be getting better.

Everywhere we went, from church to restaurants to vacations, people would always compliment us on how well we looked together. We even had a church member tell us that we should be on the cover of a magazine. I had always been attracted to Calvin. Even though my love was not as strong as it was in the beginning, I still found him to be incredibly attractive; and I did not long to be with any-one else. I never had the urge to cheat—even when I would catch him communicating inappropriately with other women. And this was quite often. He had a very difficult time resisting the innuendos from women. I think it really validated him to some degree. He com-plained that I was no longer affectionate enough, so he gravitated to them and their advances to make him feel more like a man. I can't even begin to tell you how many fights we had over this one thing. I never knew of him to actually have a physical relationship with another, but I have a strong suspicion that it happened. At any rate, the communication itself was still wrong and very hurtful. I realized that I was probably reaping what I had sown while he was away, so I took it.

Eventually, we were able to build our dream home. God was really good to us, but we seemed to only give Him praise when we were in church. I remember asking Cal several times if we could pray together. He would always say yes, but we never did—only to bless our food. That was crazy because I was singing in front of twenty thousand members at church every Sunday—and we never prayed at home. I still considered myself saved and didn't even stop to think that I was living in a backslidden state. God must have been blessing us because we were faithful, not because we kept His commandments. And He certainly wasn't blessing us because of our prayer lives. But we were still saved—and we were still on our way to heaven! To everyone on the outside, we were the perfect couple. Little did they know…

Our marriage would only last two more years after we moved into our dream home. Sex became a chore for me to the point where I began to think something was physically wrong with me. The arguments between us became much worse even to the extent of having physical altercations on a few occasions. We just continued to drift apart. I was concerned that if we did not separate, someone would eventually get hurt or even worse. Calvin, who had always been a relatively mild-tempered guy, changed. He became much more violent, impatient, and even intimidating to me. I knew he was too big and strong to allow him to continue to put his hands on me. Ironically, I never considered myself part of an abusive relationship or a victim. Perhaps it was because if I knew nothing else I knew how to fight back. It wasn't about winning with him—just surviving. I think the stresses of his company, along with the financial obligations and confusion inside the home, were more than he could handle. There were times that I really became fearful of what he was capable of doing. He would get so mad.

I felt he had stopped making us a priority. And when we both stopped, it was over. I became numb to anything he would do or say. I longed for peace in my life and in my home. I felt so bad that our girls had to be subjected to our arguments every day. They deserved so much better, but it was like we could not control ourselves. In that regard, we were horrible parents—too selfish to put their need to feel safe before our need to tear each other down. Calvin would get so loud. He had a hard time containing his emotions at times. I, on the other hand, could argue with him without the girls ever hearing a word I murmured. There have been many nights I've cried myself to sleep just thinking about how they must have felt when we were arguing, envisioning the looks on their little innocent faces. God, how could we do that to our babies? I had to get them away from all this confusion.

I remember waking up one morning after having had a fight the day before and asking myself if this was all my life was going to be. Can I actually see myself feeling this way for the rest of my life? Is this all God has for me? Calvin had stayed out until 4:00 a.m., and he was very unapologetic for it. I was honestly outdone. I filed for divorce that day and never looked back. Although he continued to text me in attempts to salvage our marriage, I had no intention of going backward. I was miserable, and I just wanted to feel happy again. When all we had was God and each other, things were good. When we allowed all of the outside distractions to consume us, we were done! We took our eyes off God, and He removed His covering from our lives. This was the end of our love story. I no longer liked him, and to me, that was worse than falling out of love with him.

Chapter 3

The Blackness

During our separation period, I was at such a peaceful place in my life. I looked forward to coming home again. And I had not felt that way in quite some time. It was more important to me that my girls knew that a home should be filled with love and peace rather than ensuring they had both parents who remained together only to fill the home with confusion. I needed to make sure they knew that arguments and fights were not the norm. I wanted them to always feel safe in their own home. I vowed I would never argue with another man in their presence after their dad—and I kept that promise.

Prior to the divorce being finalized, I did meet someone else. My girlfriend, who was a DJ on a local radio station, convinced me to create a profile on a popular dating site just to test the waters. To be completely honest, the very last thing I was thinking about was getting involved with another man. I had warded them off to a certain degree. I was enjoying the new space I was in, and I was in no hurry to disrupt my current situation. I agreed to create the profile, though, just to appease her; but I had absolutely no expectations. After a few weeks on the site, I was ready to delete my profile. All the messages started looking the same to me, and I was getting bored with it all. There was absolutely no way I could possibly respond to all the messages I was receiving. They were coming in at a much faster pace than I was moving, obviously. As I was preparing to close my account, I opened one last message. This seemingly harmless action would change the course of my life—*forever!*

His username was Blackful. His profile jumped out at me so loudly that I could hardly contain my desire to learn more about this man. I could tell he was well-spoken, polished, and adequately intelligent—mixed with a little hood. For the first time since being on the site, someone had my attention. I responded to his message with a simple "Hello" and anxiously awaited his reply. Within a matter of minutes, I received what I was waiting for. His style of communicating with me was very delicate and I liked it.

"If I may ask, what is the status of your separation?" he replied. I told him that the divorce was in motion and should be finalized within a matter of months. From there, we chose to take our communication offline, and we exchanged numbers.

It would be a few weeks later before we officially met. Although he seemed very interested, I could also tell he was very calculated and deliberate in what he chose to do. At this time, I was a regional director for a well-known national business services company. I had just left an annual function I was required to attend with them and decided to give him a call. He answered, and to my surprise, he asked if he could come pick me up for a late-night dinner. I was complaining about how bad the food was, and he obviously felt the need to ensure I went to bed with a happy stomach. I said yes and changed clothes to make sure I looked decent for our first meeting.

Shortly after, my doorbell rang—it was him—in the flesh. He looked at me and immediately said "Awe, shit!" He cuffed his mouth and had a certain look of absolute satisfaction on his face as he was saying it, so I figured he was pleased with what he saw. On the other hand, I had a slightly different reaction. Although I never let on to him, I was a little disappointed at first glance. He was just *all right* to me. He certainly didn't look as good in person as he did in his pictures. I could be overly picky and critical at times. I knew this about myself and completely owned it; however, there seemed to be nothing I could ever do to control it. At any rate, it was late, and I was hungry; so I figured, what the heck.

I actually found that I was really enjoying his company, but I wasn't feeling those butterflies I thought I would just yet. We continued to date on a pretty regular basis, and the more I knew about him, the more I liked about him. This man treated me better than anyone ever had. He gave me the strength I needed to see my divorce through to completion. He became the friend I always wanted my husband to be. This guy earned my trust very quickly; however, it took him a little longer to win my love. It wasn't because he was undeserving but rather because I had no desire to fall in love again anytime soon. I had already decided that if I was to marry again, it would be one of convenience, not love. Love just didn't seem to work for me, and I was not willing to risk getting hurt again.

This man, Blu, had a stable job working for the federal government, but clearly, that was not going to be good enough for me—not this time. I had already supported Calvin's dream of building a stable business from ground zero. This time, the man needed to already be financially independent to win me over. I had decided that I wasn't interested in budgeting for things I desired. I just wanted them to come easily. So despite the fact that I would go out with Blu on a regular basis, I was guarding my heart. And I was only dating him until someone better came along. I was forthcoming with him with regards to what I wanted; however, I feel like he only heard what he chose to hear. He never slowed down in his pursuit of me.

He taught me what it felt like to be treated like a lady. He was the most chivalrous man I had ever known. I never opened my own door of any kind in his presence. This was grounds for a major argument if I tried to. He was very accommodating and genuinely concerned for my well-being. He truly seemed to have my best interest at heart, and that felt good to me—it felt safe. I did feel, though, that I had created some insecurities within him because of how forthcoming I was about what I expected or desired in a man.

I can remember, on a few occasions, he gained access to my e-mails and discovered correspondences between me and other guys. I was telling them how fond I was of Blu but that we were not exclusive because I wanted to be with someone who was financially independent. He would delicately approach me about the e-mails as he knew how wrong he was for the intrusion into my privacy. He would talk around the subject in hopes of getting me to confess. I would finally come to realize, at some point during the conversation, that he had actually read my e-mails. This created major tension, and I would normally take a break from him for a few days as a result. He would convince me that he was acting in a way that was uncharacteristic of him based on the fact that he was so enamored with me. The fact of the matter was that I really didn't feel as though I was telling him anything different than what he was reading in my personal e-mails. Obviously, there was a huge disconnection somewhere.

I also wanted someone who looked as different from my ex as possible. I wanted no reminders of what I had. Blu fit that bill perfectly. I went from light-skinned to brown-skinned, from curly hair to long dreadlocks, and from a hefty build to a slender one. They both had their own unique swag, and neither was better than the other; but they were different, and that was good enough for me. They both possessed an innate ability to dress perfectly for any occasion. You know how you are sometimes left to wonder how a guy might show up dressed for a date? Like—will he wear a pair of hard-bottom black gators with khaki pants, and a short-sleeve polo? Or will his sneaker shoe strings be dirty? Although fashion is subjective, clearly, all of it just doesn't work. Fortunately, I never had these concerns with Cal or Blu. I was confident that whenever we stepped out, we would always represent well.

I can recall Blu telling me that he loved taking me out. When I asked him why, he said, "I love the looks on everyone's faces when I walk in with you. It's like they are all wondering how that dude got *that* girl."

I remember being flattered when he told me that—but I've since come to realize that it wasn't at all about me. It was only about him. He felt as though I made him look good, so he was willing to deal with any imperfections, shortcoming, or reservations I may have had at the time.

Blu was very protective of me. He listened to me as though what I had to say was the most important thing in the world. And he would often reply with only one word—"noted." I would often think out loud regarding something I wanted or needed to accomplish, and it would manifest in a matter of days through him. He helped pay my bills. He exposed me to things I'd never experienced as well as places I'd never seen. He was in tune with me, and he made me feel valued. He was patient with me and overlooked my imperfections. Through him, I learned what it meant to be made a true priority. He studied me hard—and ultimately mastered me. I loved how he made me feel. As much as I wanted to resist falling in love again, it was happening.

More than even me, my girls were extremely fond of him. He took out time with them and taught them things they didn't even know they had an interest in learning. They felt safe with him, and they grew to love him almost as much as they loved their own father. There were a few times he would become overjoyed on the inside because my baby girl would slip up and call him Daddy. She would quickly correct herself, but he knew he must be doing something right in order for her to feel comfortable enough with him to call him that. I knew it as well. He loved my girls, and he was good to them. This, more so than anything else, sealed the deal for me.

We had a very physical relationship. As a matter of fact, more physical than I had ever known to that point. The chemistry between us was unparalleled. He pleased me in every way—and he knew it. He was extremely unselfish in the bedroom. His pleasure came through knowing he was pleasing me. And he did just that. One thing I quickly realized was that there was nothing physically wrong with me in this area as I thought it was during the last few years of my marriage. I had simply fallen out of love with my husband. That's why sex had become such a chore for me. I spent countless nights wondering what type of ailment I had. My ob-gyn was correct—it was psychological, not physical. I knew this now more than ever!

I remember asking Blu one evening after having made love, "Do you have a personal relationship with Christ, and have you accepted Him as your Lord and Savior?" He replied with a very solemn "Yes." That was good enough for me. And never again was there any mention of it. I can't say why that was important to me since we were living in sin. It just was. He would attend church with me on Sundays and was my biggest supporter when I ministered through song. I would often ask him if he was ready to join; however, I didn't want to pressure him. He would say it wasn't the right time yet. We never prayed together, except to bless our food. Does this sound familiar? God was only a big part of my life on Sundays. I felt no guilt or shame for what I was doing. I was perfectly content to say I was saved and even think I was without including God in anything I did. I rarely asked Him for His guidance or advice. I've now come to realize that I was a religious person, not a spiritual one. I really didn't have much of a true relationship with God—I just thought I did.

During this time, Calvin went out of his way to make Blu feel uncomfortable. He asked me to set up a lunch meeting with him and Blu, so he could become familiar with this man who was spending time with his girls. I thought that was a fair request and so did Blu who adamantly stated, "I'll answer any questions he may have pertaining to my character because he deserves to know that; however, our personal relationship is none of his concern and will not be discussed."

They met and conversed over lunch. Calvin implied subtle threats the entire meeting, and although I didn't realize it at that time, they penetrated Blu. He wanted Blu to go through him prior to doing anything for his girls. And it was important to him that Blu knew he would hurt him if he ever messed over our girls in any way. Calvin knew what type of mother I was and how protective I was over our girls. He knew he could trust my judgment as it related to who I allowed around our girls, so I saw this as nothing more than a power trip and an intimidation tactic. To some degree, I think it may have worked.

I allowed Calvin to have way too much of a presence in my life after the divorce. I was trying to make things easy for him and for our girls. I never restricted him to the joint custody court order when it came to spending time with our daughters. I allowed him to see and have the girls as much as he wanted—and that was a lot in the beginning. I never took into consideration how uncomfortable it may have made Blu feel. I did, however, always have the best of intentions at heart. My girls enjoyed time spent with their dad, but they also enjoyed spending time with Blu and me. We were forming our own little family unit. It felt very natural for all of us.

Blu and I decided it was best for me to sell my current home and get something more affordable. He always stated that he never wanted to live in another man's home. He wanted us to get something untainted, so we began our search for what would be our new home. We looked diligently for months; however, as the time drew closer for us to make a decision on which home we would purchase, he started to get cold feet. He began to talk about what a serious joint venture this was and how he wasn't sure whether or not we should make the purchase together. This caught me completely off guard. I never saw this coming. He had been so consistent and steady to this point. In fact, he was rather predictable and safe for me. He didn't seem to be swaying, at all, with regards to how he felt for me. He just seemed scared to move forward with the plans we'd made about purchasing the home. To be honest, this was a turnoff to me. It made me think he was wishy-washy and a bit unstable.

I, naturally, began to put a little distance between us after this. I began to make myself less and less available. It was not in an attempt to punish him. I was just feeling differently toward him—about him. He still participated in helping me locate my new home, and when I found it, I purchased it—alone. This was a sign that warranted me to proceed with caution. The truth of the matter is that I should have paid even closer attention to it than I did. Perhaps it should have been the deal breaker, but it wasn't. Not by a long shot.

Shortly after I moved into my new home, I allowed Calvin to talk me into a trial reconciliation between us. I knew it would hurt Blu, but it was something I felt I needed to do—so I did it. I told Blu I needed some time to sort out my feelings. Unfortunately, I was not as forthcoming as I should have been about the situation. I started spending time with Calvin again prior to even telling him. I made mention to him that we needed to talk, but I was not ready to hurt him. And to be completely honest, I was still trying to convince myself that it was the right decision for me. Little did I know that he would be hurt even the more by the way I actually handled it. He began to notice that I was not answering his calls or text messages one day. It was a day that I was spending family time with Calvin and our girls. I allowed Calvin to stay at the house that night, and when he left for work the next morning, there was an immediate knock at my front door. It was Blu. I'm still not sure how long he actually waited outside my home to see who was there, but that's exactly what he did.

He witnessed Calvin leaving my home, and he was truly hurt. Although I had already begun to put space in between us, I got absolutely *no* pleasure out of knowing I was responsible for his pain. He pleaded with me to stay with him and try to work things out, but I told him I needed to follow through with my commitment to Calvin. I could feel how badly he was hurting, and it was almost more than I could bear. He asked me to meet him that evening at a hotel close to my home, so we could talk. I felt obligated to do so—it was certainly the very least I could do. I went with full intentions of just talking; however, our emotions quickly took over. He made love to me more passionately than he ever had to that point. It was more than I could handle, and I just began to weep—we both did. I was so incredibly confused. What was I doing—to my girls, to myself, and to these men? I felt dirty. I felt like I was the worst person I had ever known at that moment. I felt deep love for Blu; but I would get up, clean myself off, and go home where Calvin would be waiting for me.

That next Sunday, I had to sing at church. We went as a family again…Calvin, the girls and I. I had to lead the choir song that Sunday. Imagine my surprise when the invitation to join the church was given, and Blu answered the call that day. I couldn't believe he was actually joining *my* church. Why now? Why wait until we break up to join? Was he simply seeking attention from me? Was he trying to play on my heartstrings? Why now? Calvin wondered the same thing. He saw Blu go up for membership, and as I sat in the choir stand, I could clearly see both of them, along with the expressions on both their faces, at all times. It would be an understatement if I said it was an awkward day.

After church was over, Blu sent me a text spilling his heart to me. I was at dinner with Calvin and our girls when I received it. It brought me to tears. It was filled with so much pain and anguish. He complimented me on the song I sang then went on to tell me that it was his sincere hope that I would find my way back to him.

"Tee, I feel bad for the guy. I really do. But you and the girls were my family first. And I want you back!" Calvin stated. "I know he's hurting, but I don't think it compares to the pain I've experienced since you divorced me," he insisted.

I was truly torn. My insides just hurt. I wanted to be everything to everyone. I truly did. I wanted to fix everything and everyone. But how could I do that as broken as I was? I had begun to slip into a very dark and lonely place. I was so overwhelmed.

I tried to forget about Blu, but he would text me daily. I finally agreed to meet him one evening. We met at a quaint little sports bar in the Cumberland Mall area. We talked about how our lives were going without each other in them. I finally asked him the *question*.

"So have you slept with anyone else since we've been apart?" I asked, already confident of the answer because I imagined him staying home pining over me since we had been apart. I imagined he had been as depressed as he told me he was, so I knew there was no way he could have been with another—not already. When he answered, my heart sank to my stomach. I wasn't prepared for what would come next.

"Yes, I have, Tisa."

I knew I had no right to be angry or upset, but I was. I was so hurt, but why? I played it off as though it made no difference to me. I told him I was happy for him and the fact that he was moving on with his life. I'm sure my cover was blown, though, when he saw a tear roll down my cheek. He assured me this wasn't the case—that it just happened. He tried to convince me that it was me he loved and that the incident meant nothing to him. We parted ways. He went wherever it was he went that night, and I went home to Calvin.

As the next few days went by, I started feeling as though I had made the wrong decision. I knew I was no longer in love with Calvin—more now than ever before. I began to feel as though I was literally suffocating in my own home. I thought about Blu more and more each passing day. I started to feel fearful—that someone else was going to win his heart if I didn't get my act together. I knew I had to make a decision before it was too late. I never prayed over the decision. I never consulted with God nor did I ask Him to direct my path. Again, I just did what I thought was best for me. I did what I thought would make me happy. I sat Calvin down and told him I just could not do this anymore. As much as I wanted to salvage my family, it was just too late. I was emotionally disconnected. I told him I felt like I was suffocating, and I had to get myself back to a good place. I had experienced what it felt like to really start living again—what it felt like to be made the top priority in someone's life—and I was not willing to give that up. It was then I realized I was really in love with Blu.

Although Calvin was really hurt, I had decided that I would no longer put his feelings before my own. I had spent the last several years of our marriage getting in wherever he decided he wanted to fit me in to his life. I never felt safe or protected with him—not the way a wife should feel. I was placed behind everyone in his life—mother, sisters, cousins, and friends. Why in the world would I choose to go back to that? The thought of it made me angry, so I had to hold on to that feeling long enough to do what was best for me this time. I convinced myself that it was time for me to be selfish. It was time for me to put my wants and needs first. And that's just what I did.

I called Blu and told him I needed to see him to which he quickly agreed. I went to his place and told him about the decision I had made. "I love you, Blu. I think I'm just realizing how much I actually do. I'm completely committed to making us work if you'll have me back." He did not hesitate. In fact, his answer came in the form of him making passionate love to me for hours. I felt happy again, and things appeared to be back to my new normal. I often wondered if he fought so hard for me because he truly loved me or because his ego couldn't take him losing to another man. He had always tried to assure me that he did not have an ego, but I soon learned different—much different.

After several months, Blu and I decided it would be best for him to move in with me and the girls. We were already spending every day together, so why not combine our incomes and make things easier for us? Things were good, initially—very good. He exposed me to a whole new world. He took me to places I had only dreamt of going. He was a very culturally-polished, well-spoken, and self-edu-

49

cated man. He challenged me intellectually and stimulated me physically as no other man ever had before. He studied my every move. He learned me like a book. Then he responded as he knew I needed him to respond. Many of my friends saw this as manipulation. I saw it as love.

I often complained to my ex-husband that he was selfish. Many of his decisions were based on what made him happy first. I hated that about him. But Blu presented himself as the most selfless person I had ever known. He did very little without first consulting me. We made decisions together, and that felt good to me. He made me feel secure in the fact that he had only my best interest at heart. He was very soft spoken. Many times, I would have to ask him to repeat himself because he talked so softly. He placed me before his family, his friends—everything. And even though he had a daughter whom he loved dearly, I always felt that my girls and I were his first priority. He was everything I never had.

There was very little that anyone could have told me about him which I would have believed. I began to put my trust in him as I should have only put in God. This man was literally my world. And this was all new to me. I had loved before. I had even loved hard before. But trust me when I say I had *never* loved any man the way I loved him. His imperfections, and there were many, became invisible to me. I began to overlook everything he did. I was losing my voice and myself in my attempts to love him. He had successfully convinced me that no one cared for me as much as he did—that no one had my back as he did.

I can recall one night as we were cuddling. I asked him a question that seemed to catch him off guard. "Why would any woman ever let you go?"

He was stunned by the question and replied, "Why do you ask that?"

I told him I couldn't imagine anyone wanting to be without him once they were with him. "When it comes to a real man, you seem to be almost perfect! What woman wouldn't want to be with you?" I asked.

He assured me that he was far from perfect but that he gives of himself freely to the woman he loves. He then made me a promise—

one that would prove impossible for him to keep. "Tisa, if you'll just give me your heart, I promise to always protect it. If you'll just love me, I promise to always love you back." I was a bit guarded, so little did he know I was already in by that time.

Don't get me wrong. I knew this guy had his faults. They were just not deal breakers for me. I was confident that they paled in comparison to what I had dealt with in my marriage. I remember coming home from work unexpectedly one day only to find him looking at porn on his computer. He quickly shut the laptop down, so I couldn't see what he was viewing. "Pull it back up, Blu. I wanna see what you're looking at." My request was soft and not confrontational, so he reluctantly did what I asked. He had no idea how I would react, but I was good. My choice would have been that he *not* choose to look at it; however, I figured that someone who was as freaky as he was in the bedroom absolutely *must* be getting tips from somebody. He freely did things to my body that no other man had before. He aimed to please me in every way—and he did. He was the very best lover I'd ever had! His fetish for porn was not healthy. I knew it, but I dismissed it. As long as he was good to me, as long as he didn't cheat on me, and as long as he put me first, I was good. I was okay with it.

Many of my girlfriends didn't care for him at all. Some thought he was arrogant. Others thought he was a master manipulator who wanted to alienate me from the rest of the world, so he could have me all to himself. Although I was curious about why they saw him that way, it never truly bothered me—until my sister told me how she felt. Initially, she really seemed to take to him—as did my mother. But as time progressed, I noticed that she had really become very cold and standoffish toward him. It was very apparent, so I know that as perceptive as he was, he felt it too. He would compliment her or try to make small talk, and she would always reply with very dry remarks. I finally asked her one day why the sudden change in her communication with him. Her response floored me.

She said, "Tee, I can't put my finger on it, but there's something about that Motherfucker I just don't like! I just don't trust him!" Although I defended him to her, silently, her comments really bothered me. I would proceed with one eyebrow raised from then on.

Then one day, completely out of the blue, I discovered that he was flawed. By this, I mean I discovered that he wasn't as honest, forthcoming, integral, and committed as I was led to believe he was. I became *aware* that he was not without fault—that he was human just like me—if not worse. And when he knew I knew—he changed. One morning, he left for work and mistakenly left one of his two cell phones at the house. I had never felt a need to doubt what he told me. I trusted him completely, but for some reason, I made the decision to look through his phone. To this day, I have no idea what prompted me to do so. I have to believe it was the Holy Spirit. I wasn't feeling, in any way, insecure about him or us. I was just being nosy—seeing what I could find. And what I found would change the course of our relationship forever!

I saw this particular number numerous times in his text message threads, so I opened the messages up only to discover that he had sent a few *dick pics* to someone and stated in the message that they were for her eyes only. I absolutely could not believe what I was seeing. Not him! Anyone but him! He was too classy and reserved to do anything like this. Not to mention he was supposed to be head over heels in love with me! I noticed the pics were sent during the time that we were separated which gave me a little bit of relief. But who was he communicating with on this level? Who would this man, as reserved as he was, feel comfortable enough sending pics like this to? He had assured me that his one-time fling was nothing at all significant, and that the woman had basically seduced him into sleeping with her. He made it seem as though she had thrown herself all over him. He was very adamant about this fact. I didn't know who it was, but I was determined to find out.

I finished getting ready for work, and on my way I, called my close DJ girlfriend to tell her what I had discovered. Her local celebrity status often allowed others to feel comfortable talking to her about things they may not normally be forthcoming about. She asked me to give her the number and allow her to make the call for me. I wasn't hurt or even mad—just disappointed and aware. I was beginning to wonder how well I really knew this guy. Until now, he never gave me a reason to be suspicious of him or his intent. I agreed to let my girlfriend handle the situation, and I proceeded on to work. She called me a few hours later and told me that she had a very long conversation with the woman and that she had been very cooperative. It was Blu's ex-girlfriend of four years. Someone he claimed to have no lingering feelings for or dealings with.

She expressed an interest to my girlfriend in speaking with me directly. She asked my friend to have me call her, so I did just that. She was very warm and inviting. There were no hidden innuendos nor was there any evidence of any condescending undertones. She was genuinely interested in learning who I was and answering any questions I may have had for her. Apparently, she and Blu made an attempt to rekindle what they had during the time of our separation. Her story differed from his drastically. They had spent many intimate nights together not just the one that he spoke of. She was still very much in love with him at this time. She did say that she figured he was with someone else now because he just disappeared after a couple of months. He stopped calling her or returning her calls. I assumed this is when he and I got back together.

She told me some things about him that really caught me off guard. While I had always considered him to be the *best* boyfriend I had ever had, she claimed he was her worst. Although she was still deeply in love with him, she said he had a very dark side. She told me of the time her family and friends hosted an intervention for her in attempts to get her away from him. Apparently, he was mentally and also physically abusive to her. She was a principal, and she told me of the time he got so angry that he grabbed her by her neck, choking her at one of her school's football games—all in front of all her students and colleagues. There was something about her voice—she was believable. I remember feeling sorry for her. I thought that, certainly, she must be a weak woman to allow *any* man this much power over her. I knew she had to be telling the truth; however, I did not know this man she spoke of. He did not sound even remotely familiar to me. But I would meet him—eventually.

When I finally responded to his phone calls later that day, I shared with him what I had discovered. I told him everything that had transpired that day. He was not happy about it at all. His cover had been blown. Up until this point, he had me convinced that he was damn near perfect in every way. He would always tell me that he had never done anything to dishonor our relationship. He had me thinking and believing that every misfortune that happened between us was my fault. And until that point, I truly believed most of it probably was. I was just out of a fourteen-year relationship and a thirteen-year marriage. I was no stranger to dysfunction, and it certainly *had my number on speed dial.* I was never in denial of this; however, my blinders were removed this day. I started to see him for who he truly was, and he never wanted that to happen.

When he knew that I actually could see him, he changed. More than anything else, he was disappointed that his true colors were revealed. He stopped trying as hard as he had before. It was almost as if the wind had been knocked out of him. He possessed classic symptoms of a narcissistic person. He took very little ownership of his wrongdoings but was very quick to pinpoint others'. Although I saw him in a different light, I was still convinced that he couldn't possibly be as bad as she made him out to be, so, as stupid as I must have been, I was willing to take my chances with him. It took us a few weeks to get past what had transpired, but we did. We decided that we would put it behind us and move forward.

I began to notice that he would drink a bit heavier. I don't know if this was actually the case or if I was just more aware of him doing it now. It never really posed a problem. It was just an observation initially. I knew he enjoyed sipping on his Hennessy and Coke—and it was okay with me. However, one evening, he had been drinking a lot. I was doing my baby girl's hair in our bedroom, and unbeknownst to me, he had picked up my cell phone and proceeded to go through it thoroughly. He had done this several times before just as he had hacked my e-mail account from time to time. This particular night, he came across some very innocent text messages between me and a cop friend I had developed a close relationship with prior to meeting him.

We met when I was married. He handled a fraud case with the company I was working for at that time. The relationship was an inappropriate one as we were both married, but it was not a sexual one, so I told myself it was okay. I knew he had grown to love me; and I cared for him as well, but I was able to keep things in their proper perspective. As I stated, it was never a sexual relationship; but it was an emotional one. He was my friend and my confidant. I could tell him anything without fear of judgment or ridicule. This did not set well with Blu, so I ended the regular communications with him when I decided to commit to Blu. I didn't need the confusion. Besides, I understood where he was coming from, and I suppose I would have felt the same.

The text messages that day were completely innocent, though. He was actually just reaching out to see how I was doing as he would from time to time. He did, however, tell me on numerous occasions prior to that that he did not feel Blu was good for me. He would say his gut just told him that this guy was bad for me. I ignored his advice because I just figured he was a little jealous. He admitted he was but that he also wanted the best for me, and he didn't feel this guy was the one. Anyway, when Blu saw the messages from him, he did not take them well. He was not, at all, an argumentative guy. As a matter of fact, I always loved the fact that he was a rather soft-spoken man. I knew when he spoke, he had something significant to say. Although we never argued in front of our kids, we came close to it that day. I made it clear to him in the beginning of our relationship that that was a deal breaker for me. If my girls were ever made to feel their mother was unsafe in any way, I would walk away and never look back. They heard enough arguments and fights to last them a lifetime when I was with their dad. I promised myself and them that they would never experience anything but peace in our home going forward—and I meant just that.

He was drunk and mad, though. That was not a good combination for him. He was picking with me as I was doing my baby girl's hair. "Awe come on now Tisa, certainly you have nothing to hide right?" I assured him that I did not as I continued brushing my baby's hair. "Just give me the phone back. You've obviously seen all you need to." I said a bit jokingly, as I did not want to alarm my baby girl. I wanted her to think we were having a very light-hearted conversation. He responded with "I assure you that when I am finished with your phone, you will be the first to know." Although I was getting a bit concerned about his current state of mind, I looked at him with a smile on my face, never getting up from my seat and very calmly said "We are not going to argue about this…not now." As he proceeded to walk away, he said loudly "Yeah girls, this is who your mom's been fucking since we've been together."

I could not believe he would say something like that for my girls to hear. I was so upset, but I downplayed it because I did not want them to become overly concerned. I knew he had gone out to the front porch, and I thought it best that I let him cool down for a bit before approaching him. I was satisfied to learn that my girls didn't even hear the comment he had made. They felt safe in his presence, and they were in their own little worlds in our home.

I put the baby girl to bed, and the oldest was in her room where she enjoyed staying most of the time, anyway. She was at the stage in her life where she was concerned only with what was going on in her circle. I was glad about that this day. I went downstairs and out to the front porch where he was. An argument ensued, and he broke my phone into several pieces. "Tisa, why the *fuck* are you still communicating with this man? I'm here everyday with you and these girls doing everything I can to show you how much I love you…and this is what you do!" By this time I was pissed because he had just destroyed my phone…my lifeline. I didn't feel the need to offer any explanations beyond what I already had. I mean, clearly he could see the conversation was completely innocent and certainly random. "Just leave, Blu. You have really tried me tonight!" Although I could see that, beneath the liquid courage that had overtaken him, he was really hurting, I just didn't care by this time. I was pissed and I would ride it out all night. He was familiar with my temper, my family his-tory…my dysfunction. And usually, he wanted no parts of it. This night was different though.

He was acting in a way that I had never seen before, and I actu-ally became a little fearful of what he may have been capable of doing to me. I called the police from my home phone, and they came and removed him from the home that night. I told him the next day that he needed to leave, so he moved out. He was very angry with me.

Again, according to him, this was all my fault. There was a part of me that believed him because I always thought about how good he was in the beginning of our relationship. I blamed myself for messing things up, and I would spend the next two years trying to get back that man I had fallen in love with. But he was gone—for good. I saw bits and pieces of him periodically, but that was it.

After a few months, we began seeing each other again. There was a stronghold on me now. I couldn't seem to leave him alone. And when we were not together, I was sad—very sad. He would go through something very similar with me to the point of him not being able to go to work for days when we would break up. There was something very dysfunctional and demonic about our unhealthy relationship. At times, it just felt dark. We always said that when things were good, it didn't get any better; however, when they were bad, there was nothing worse. But that guy I initially met was like crack to me. I had to do whatever I could to get that guy back. I wanted that same feeling again in my life. I would stop at nothing to get him back. Rejection became common place for me. He rejected me time after time with ease. This was when I came to realize that I had completely lost myself in him. He was the first man to ever reject me…to discount me. I hated the way it made me feel, but I had to have him so I took it. I would plead with him to give our love another try…not to give up on us. His response was always the same one "Love is not our issue." How did this happen? I went from feeling as though I had all the control in our relationship, all the power…to *this*. At times, I felt stripped of all power, significance and even value and self worth.

We both would go out with other people when we broke up in an attempt to get over each other. That became our norm. There was simply no one who could replace us to each other. We ended up leaving a trail of hurt people in our attempts to get over one another. I guess it's true what they say, "Hurt people really do hurt people." I don't care how deeply we seemed to be involved with someone else. As soon as one of us made contact with the other, that new relationship was over. We would not ask each other very many questions when we reconciled as we both knew we probably didn't want to hear the answers. We would just try to pick up right where we left off. This happened several times with us. It was a battle of power with us. Instead of us using our strengths to help one another through the weaknesses, we used them to tear the other down. It always seemed that when one of us was strong, the other was weak. We were becoming very comfortable living in our own very sad dysfunction.

We loved entertaining together…and we were good at it. We were always throwing some holiday party, and our circle of friends enjoyed gathering with us. We threw a New Year's Eve party during our third year of being together. There was already a slight bit of tension between us because of what he purchased me for Christmas. We had always gone all out for one another on special occasions. This particular year, I had purchased him a couple of suits along with all the fixings. He was really surprised and very appreciative of the gift, and that pleased me. However, when I opened my gift, I was a bit disappointed. I felt it was extremely impersonal, and I was not happy. It was a wine chiller. I felt like that was equivalent to something he bought me during our very first month of dating. And I would have been happy to get it any other time, but I was expecting more for Christmas. Although I smiled and said thank you, I made him aware of my disappointment the next day and the next day—and the next.

For this, I was just wrong. I came across like a spoiled brat who was pouting because things weren't to my liking. I was critical of him for getting me something so practical and simple. But why? I told him I was embarrassed to tell my girlfriends what he had purchased me for Christmas. He took it all in stride, but of course, I knew it bothered him to some degree. So at our New Year's Eve party, as all my girlfriends were talking about what they received, I made the ultimate mistake. I made light of the gift he got me in front of everyone—and this emasculated him. He was deeply hurt and even a bit angry with me. What I would learn a few weeks later was almost enough to spiral me downward—into a very dark place.

My cousin, who had actually attended our party, called me and revealed to me that Blu had an engagement ring in his pocket that night and couldn't bring himself to propose after I embarrassed him as I did. My heart sank to my stomach at that moment. I literally got sick when he told me this. And obviously, most of our friends who were there knew about it and expected it to happen. By this time, I certainly felt like he was the man I wanted to spend the rest of my life with. And I knew he didn't see himself living his life without me in it. At the end of the day, this man had very serious issues when it came to marriage—and many other things. He would always make light of the time he spent in therapy after ending his previous relationship by saying "I always say that everybody can benefit from a little couch time." He had been forthcoming to me about this dark period in his life, and I never judged him for it.

There was always an excuse as to why he couldn't make that ultimate commitment again, though. Most times, he would reference his mother and say that he was terrified of repeating her mistakes in judgment—married and divorced five times. What I realized at that point, though, was that perhaps I wasn't ready or even deserving of a proposal then. I knew God couldn't possibly have been pleased with me and the lifestyle I was living.

One particular morning, we were talking about going our separate ways. He was going to see his daughter and stated he would get the items he had brought to my home after he returned the next day. I went out with my sorority sisters that evening and stayed out pretty late. He was not used to me being out because we were generally together. He had access to my home even though he no longer stayed there. He began texting me around midnight making hefty claims about me being with another man because I was not at home. I kept asking him why he was at my home instead of being with his daughter. In short, he had come back early to check up on me. To his surprise, I was out having a good time without him. And he didn't like it.

I just started ignoring his messages and continued having a good time. I told him to leave my home and lock up after himself. I arrived home around 2:00 a.m. and was surprised to see my garage door was up, and the door leading into my home was wide open. I went in and found Blu as I had never seen him before. It was obvious he had been drinking, but he was completely irate. He was out of his mind because of his private thoughts about me. He was obviously convinced that I had been out with another man, and there was no convincing him otherwise. He became violent, choking me, and pushing me and calling me all kinds of obscenities. He grabbed me around my neck and lifted me off the floor, slamming my head into a picture I had on my wall and breaking the frame. I broke loose and ran to the kitchen to get a knife. I was absolutely sure he was going to try to kill me that night. I had never seen that look in his eyes—and I was scared of him for the very first time. Everything his ex told me about him replayed in my mind. I was truly scared for my life.

As I held the knife out in front of me, I yelled, "Blu, I don't wanna hurt you, but if you come any closer, I'll kill you!" He proceeded to walk directly into the knife, pressing his body up against it. He said, "Go ahead and kill me. If I can't be with you, I would rather be dead."

I was terrified at this point because I was dealing with someone who felt he had nothing to lose. I picked up my house phone to call the police, but he grabbed it and smashed it into several pieces. He had already busted my cell phone earlier as I walked in the door. I remember thinking—*Is this how I'm going to die?* I had no desire to use this knife; but I knew if I had to, I would. I didn't want to spend the rest of my life in prison away from my girls. God—am I going to die tonight? Am I going to be forced to make a decision that could possibly cost me my freedom? All these thoughts were pounding in my head, and my adrenalin was on one hundred! This man really did have a dark side—very dark, and he was good at hiding it until he just couldn't. How could I not see this 'til now? I had completely ignored every sign. It was time for me to start thinking. It had become a matter of life or death.

I began trying to calm him down. I knew I had to make him feel comfortable with me again. I started telling him that we could work this out. I told him I would not call the cops nor would I leave him. I had so many mixed emotions, but all I could think of at the moment was survival—period. He eventually carried me upstairs to the bedroom where he cradled me in his arms all night long. Each time I moved, he pulled me to him even tighter. I knew it was to ensure I wouldn't try to leave and get help. I eventually drifted off but not until he made me feel safe again. The next morning, he wanted to talk. He began to tell me how this isolated incident was completely outside his character and that he had never done this before. He told me that he just loved me so much that he felt like he was losing himself. He was very convincing. My emotions were all over the place. I told him that we should take a break. That I was terrified of the possibility of this happening again.

He pleaded with me to stay. He was so adamant about the fact that this wasn't him. "Tisa, this is the first time anything like this has ever happened with me. It's completely out of my true character. Can you please just think of the type of man I've been to this point? Please don't leave me, Tisa. I can't lose you." Eventually, I fell for it all—hook, line, and sinker. We would spend the entire day together becoming comfortable with each other again. And eventually, it was as though it had never happened. I never thought to pray to God for guidance. I had completely left Him out of everything. I acted as though I no longer needed Him. It was so easy to forget the extreme feelings of fear I'd had just the night before. He made me trust him all over again. Can you imagine how differently my life would have been had I truly learned to trust God as much as I trusted my man?

The so-called isolated incidents like this one continued to happen over the next two years. Our relationship was just beyond dysfunctional. It got to the point where we didn't even attempt to hide it from our friends anymore. We would be on display for all to survey. The flip side to this, though, was that he would push me to the point of no return, then when I would act out, he would act as though he was the victim when others were around. They never saw the side of him that he showed me at home. They only saw me acting out—and a few times, I did just that! My temper had grown out of control when it came to him. And although I had allowed him to frighten me the first time he assaulted me, he knew I was no longer afraid. I would *not* be anyone's victim. In many ways, I had become the aggressor. After one of these "isolated incidents," I remember him asking me if he could make light of the fight we had just had. "Sure." I replied, having no idea what would come next. He just looked at me, shook his head and said very comically "You ain't no easy win

Nigga." Although not proud of it, I knew he was telling the absolute truth. I fought back with everything I had in me. That's what we were raised to do…fight!

Each time we would break up, I would look to Calvin to make me feel better about myself—to validate me. I can even remember having them both in the home at the same time. After one particular breakup, I had allowed Cal to move back in to help cover the bills. Blu would come to visit me while he was there. I was cuddled up with Blu on the sofa as Calvin roamed around the house. My mother was visiting at this time, and she acknowledged how awkward and uncomfortable the entire situation was. I felt extremely uncomfortable as well because I knew it was hurting Calvin. By this time, though, I was in a very dark place. You see, I had slipped into a very deep depression. I saw no light at the end of the tunnel.

I think it was the compilation of different events that caused this—delayed grief, finally dealing with the fact that my brother was really gone and *never* coming back, a failed marriage, job loss, loss of my dream home, and, to top it off, I was starting to feel like a failure in my current relationship. All these things hit me at once like a ton of bricks. I just couldn't take it anymore. It was as if the walls were closing in on me. I felt completely lifeless. I broke. And when I broke, I broke *badly*!

The company I worked for making a six-figure salary had acquired one of our top competitors. They agreed to place some of the local executives in our territory which meant the ones in place (including me) would be expected to relocate to other regions across the country in an effort to teach our newly-acquired sister company how we did business. They asked me to relocate to Knoxville, Tennessee to run that area. They really had my best interest at heart by asking me to move back home. They knew I had recently divorced and figured I would have a great support system there. I was torn because I felt guilty over moving the girls so far away from their dad. After all, I was already the bad guy for divorcing him in the first place. I needed help making this decision. I needed to get Blu's opinion. I had grown to trust his advice, and I needed it then. When I told Blu I was considering relocating back home for the job, he dropped to his knees, began to sob, and begged me not to leave him. So I stayed. I negotiated a respectable severance package and walked away. Epic mistake!

I accepted a new job in between jobs just to supplement my income 'til something better came along. And I was in my dark place. I was overwhelmed with how horrible my life was at the moment. I would become so incredibly overwhelmed with feelings of sadness until I would have to leave my job several times a day just to go outside and cry. I simply could not hold back the tears. I absolutely could not believe this was the life I had chosen for myself. How did I get here? How do I get back to the person I was? Never had I let a relationship or circumstances consume me to the point of feeling hopeless. I never understood depression. I thought it was an indication of extreme weakness in people. Mind over matter is what I used to say—until it happened to me.

I would be in the choir stand at church and be sobbing so loudly and uncontrollably until I felt embarrassed. I wanted to stop, but I couldn't. I was so incredibly broken. I would go home and want to do absolutely nothing aside from going to my room, pulling the shades, going to bed, and crying myself to sleep. I felt like such a failure—in everything. How in the world did this girl who once had it all get to this place? I literally felt as though I was dying inside. Happiness never visited me anymore. I could be in a room full of people yet feel so lonely.

I remember finally feeling like I had to tell my mother. Until now, I tried very hard *not* to talk about this or share how I was feeling with anyone but God. Funny thing—I needed Him now. It was about 3:00 a.m., and I could *not* stop balling. The kids were asleep as I never broke down in front of them. I called my mom and stepdad, who happens to be a pastor, to pray for me. I broke down and told them everything. I told them that I thought I was losing my mind. That I couldn't function throughout the day without breaking down and crying. That I have never felt constant pain like this before. And that I saw no light at the end of my tunnel. I was in an awful state. So much so, my mom got out of bed at that moment in the middle of the night and drove three hours to Atlanta to see about her child. OMG! I was in horrible shape.

My mom stayed a few days with me as I didn't even feel as though I could properly take care of my kids. The second morning she was there, I remember getting up early to take the kids to school. As soon as I pulled back into my garage, I just started wailing. I knew I needed to get it all out before I went back inside the house. I figured my mother wouldn't hear me because she was inside, so far away. In no time, she was in the garage pulling me out of my car. She immediately made me an appointment to see my primary care physician that day. I was dealing with something much deeper than I was capable of handling.

My doctor was a very conservative, relatively young white woman. She had to be my same age or a little younger. But she was so incredibly smart and good at what she did. As I was telling her how I had been feeling that day, she began giving me all the medical reasons and terminology she could muster up in an effort to help me understand what I was experiencing. As I sat there listening to all the words that were coming out of her mouth, I began to think about the fact that my mom would be leaving the very next day. I instantly began to feel extremely overwhelmed. And it happened—again! I just broke, right there—in her office—uncontrollably—again! At that time, my doctor did something I will never forget. She laid down her stethoscope alongside all her medical largo, laid her hands on me, and said, "It's time to pray." She began to pray over my body and over my mind. She spoke life into my dead spirit. She declared into the atmosphere that I would live and not die and that when God brought me through this, I would have a testimony that would be able to deliver others who were experiencing the same ordeal.

I could not believe what she was doing. I mean, I never told her I was a Christian. I certainly didn't feel as though I was living the lifestyle that would allow others to see Christ in me. I was in a backslidden state and had been for quite some time. I had become very comfortable in it. So much so, that the only time I ever felt His presence was when I ministered through song on Sundays at my church. But she saw Him in me. She saw Christ's spirit in me—through all the garbage that was piled on top of it, she still saw it. Her spirit bore witness with mine and with my mother's. She was obedient to the Holy Spirit, and she prayed for me that day. After she finished, I would never look at her as just my doctor again. She was my friend— my sister. And I loved her with all my heart.

She prescribed me the meds I needed for anxiety, depression, and insomnia while allowing God to complete His perfect work in me. For the first time in months, I felt hopeful. I felt like there actually could be at least a small glimmer of light at the end of my tunnel. I felt as though I was on the road to recovery. And although I was, it was a long hard road. She had explained to me that the type of depression I was experiencing was brought on by negative situations or occurrences that took place in my life. It was not a form of manic depression—this gave me hope. So over the course of the next year or so, when problems would arise between Blu and me, I would digress a bit, but I recognized what it was. I was like a puppet on a string by this time and so was he. We had both mastered pulling each other's strings to get reactions. The relationship had become extremely dysfunctional to the point of seemingly no return. I still wasn't strong enough to walk away though—not yet.

This continued on until *that* Sunday morning. I went to church heavyhearted even though I had to minister in song for both services that day. I remember thinking, *God, there is absolutely no way I'm gonna be able to get through this choir song today.* How in the world am I going to be able to lead a song today? I just knew I was going to break down on the stage in front of twenty thousand people. I came very close to asking our minister of music, who happened to also be our First Lady, if we could change the choir song at the last minute. I cried the entire way to the church that day; however, by the time I got there, I felt as though things would be okay.

I proceeded to sing in both services, and God was certainly glorified. It amazed me—the amount of grace and unmerited mercy He had for me—especially when I did not deserve it. He still allowed His anointing to fall fresh on me when I ministered. I never understood why He would until He spoke it into my spirit years later. He was very clear in letting me know that His anointing wasn't for me. It was for someone else who needed to hear Him through me. I was just a vessel He needed to use in order to win souls into His kingdom. This is no different than how Satan can use saved people, at times, to do ungodly things for him.

After I sang in the second service, I became overwhelmingly depressed. Satan was waiting for me as soon as I returned back to the choir stand. Bishop began to deliver the Word, and I began to just wail—right there—uncontrollably—again! My crying was a distraction to others this Sunday. I knew it, and I wanted to stop, but I couldn't. I just could not stop crying—loudly. Bishop must have heard me because he stopped right in the middle of his message and said these words.

"I have a word for someone in this service today. There is a spirit of depression in this place. But I'm here to let you know that God has a Word for you. Depression is a very selfish disease." Those words got my attention long enough for me to hear what he had to say. I mean, how was he going to quantify such a blanket statement made? I *knew* I wasn't a selfish person and never had been. So I needed to see how he backed up this statement. He proceeded to say, "When you are going through depression, you are totally and completely consumed with yourself. Woe is me. My relationship isn't what it should be. I lost my job. My children are acting out. No one cares for me. It's all about you. But I came to tell you today that as soon as you make the decision to take the focus off of self and begin to focus on helping someone who is in worse shape than you are, depression must *immediately* flee!"

God allowed me to hear him so clearly. Many people had said many things in attempts to bring me out of my dark place, but nothing penetrated my spirit until this day. That day, at that moment, I was instantly delivered from that dark disease. I immediately began to make it a point to focus on others I could help in any way—big or small. Depression no longer had me bound. I truly thank God for speaking to me through my bishop. I could not hear Him any other way up to that point, so He sent me an angel here on earth to deliver a strong Word to me.

Now let me clarify something for you. Just because I was delivered from depression certainly does not mean that I haven't experienced any bad days since. It does not mean that I don't sometimes feel down. It simply means that I no longer choose to stay there. When I felt sadness beyond that point, I would remember the words God spoke through my bishop that day; and it would bring me back. I never again experienced those feelings of hopelessness. I could always see light at the end of any situation I may have been in.

I was, at times though, consumed with guilt about the way I had treated Blu in the beginning of our relationship. He was good to me, but I wasn't ready for what he had to offer at that time. By the time I finally came to realize just how much I truly did love him, the entire dynamics of our relationship had changed. At this point in our relationship, I found myself working very hard in an effort to get him to change back into the man I first met—the man he was in the beginning. What I didn't know then was that I was ultimately wasting my time. That guy was dead—at least toward me. And he was perfectly comfortable allowing me to absorb all the blame for everything that went wrong in our relationship. It was becoming exhausting to me.

I had made the decision that if Blu and I could not get things together by our four-year mark, I would walk away and try to never look back. The date was fast approaching, and nothing seemed to be getting better. We were in counseling at our church, but it seemed as though we were only using the advice and counsel we received against each other. It was a chance for us to utilize someone else to control the actions of one another. By now, it was just a power struggle. Each time I seemed strong enough to walk away, he was weak. And when he was strong, I was the weak one. It was really a quite sad and pathetic display. We played on each other's emotions for our own personal gain, and I recognized it for what it was. I was just tired. We had completely lost ourselves trying to love each other.

As one last ditch effort, we gathered at the home of some friends for a social gathering. There were a few married couples we hung out with from time to time. Our relationship had become the topic of conversation. Everyone was asking questions in an effort to help us, but I was pretty numb at that point. Out of nowhere, Blu broke down in tears. "You all have no idea just how much I want my relationship with Tisa to work. I just don't know how. I don't know what to do. Somebody please help me. I love this woman. Help us!" It was quite a sight. I wanted to console him, but I couldn't. I was literally numb. I still loved him with all my heart, but I knew it was time for us to make a clean break. I had abruptly ended our premarital counseling sessions at the church without his input or consent. I knew it needed to be over. I felt like I was regaining my power and I liked the way it felt.

I ended things in August of 2011, and it was one of the hardest decisions I'd ever made. I had lost my father in a car accident a few months earlier, and Blu had been there for me like no other. Whether it was for appearances or because he really loved me, I will probably never know; however, we had a way of pulling together through some pretty rough times. I will always remember that day. I was at work and it was rather hectic this particular day. I was in my office when I saw my father calling me. This wasn't uncommon as he called me just about every day just to check on me and tell me he loved me. I said to myself "I know daddy doesn't want anything, so I'll just call him back later." After work, I met up with a friend to celebrate her birthday at a nice seafood restaurant in Atlanta. Shortly after arriving, my phone began to ring. It was my sister. "T, have you talked to Mama?" she asked. "No…if she called I didn't hear the phone ring." I answered. I could tell my sister was upset as she continued on. "Daddy was in a car accident and I think something really bad has happened to him." I asked her why she felt that way. "This just feels too familiar, T. Mama is saying we need to come home now." This was the same call we had received many years earlier from our mother after our brother was killed in a car accident.

I started reassuring my sister that this was not the case. There was nothing in my mind that would even allow me to believe the very same thing was now happening with our father. There was just no way. "Nikie, calm down! Daddy may have been in an accident, but I assure you he is *not* dead."

I hung up the phone and immediately called my mother. "Mama, is daddy ok?" She hesitated for a moment then said "He's been involved in a pretty bad accident. I think you and your sister should come home to see about him." I persisted, "But is he ok?" Her response was well thought out as she did not want to upset me. "Tisa, I just received a call from the hospital, and they won't give me that information over the phone; however, I think you both need to come home now." I was convinced that my dad was fine. I mean, if she was only given limited information, I was not going to assume the worse. Little did I know she already knew my dad was dead. I told her to call me back after she got to the hospital, and I would just plan on coming in the next morning.

I continued to eat dinner and tried not to think about it. I refused to allow myself to think that something was seriously wrong with my dad. I almost felt like if I didn't acknowledge it, then it would just go away. It seems rather harsh and insensitive when I think back on how I responded, but I didn't feel I could handle anything tragic happening to my dad. This was obviously my way of coping. If he was really gone, I didn't want to know, in hopes of making it go away, I suppose.

A few minutes later, my phone rang again. This time it was Calvin, my ex-husband. When I looked down and saw his number, I immediately knew my dad was gone. I felt it in the pit of my stomach…and I got angry. There was such a sense of urgency in his voice. "Tisa, I need to come and get you. Where are you?" I responded very coldly, "You need to come and get me for what?" He went on, "I just spoke to your mother." I responded "And?" After that, he just broke down and started to cry loudly. Calvin and my father were very close, even after our divorce. He always acknowledged my dad as being the first man to really show him love and affection. He was my father's son…not son-in-law.

"Calvin, are you telling me my dad is dead? Is that seriously what you're trying to tell me?" I asked in disbelief. "Yeah, T. He's gone!" I don't remember very much after that. I felt as though I was in a twilight zone. Blu came to the restaurant to pick me up. He took a week off work and took me home to lay my father to rest. During this time, I remembered my father had called me that day before he died. I finally listened to his message…

"Hey honey. This is your dad. I just want you to know that you mean more to me than life itself. I love you."

I'll never forget that message. *Never!*

Blu was there for me. He comforted me. He listened to me. He made me feel as though I could make it through this very rough period in my life. I think that perhaps it started out as a very strong love for one another that eventually turned into a relationship of complete control and manipulation. When I ended things, he became very bitter towards me. It is my opinion that he was bound and determined to repay me for the breakup—and so he did! And he did it as only he could—in true Blu fashion. His desire to ruin me, to hurt and manipulate me, was far greater than any amount of love he'd ever had for me. It was obvious.

He blamed me for everything that went wrong in our relationship. He was livid over the fact that I made the decision to stop premarital counseling. And had I actually seen progress, I would not have. We would go through a session and leave seemingly worse than when we went. We would, often times, even quote our bishop during disagreements. His response to my concerns over the way he viewed marriage would be, "Change is a process, not an event—Bishop Bronner."

I would often reply with, "The best indicator of future behavior is past behavior—Bishop Dale C. Bronner!"

We would use our own shepherd's words against each other for our own selfish gain instead of applying his words of wisdom to our own lives.

A few weeks after I ended the relationship, I had one of the biggest shocks of my life. I was forty-one, single, and now—three weeks pregnant! How could we have allowed this to happen? How could I have allowed this to happen? By now, surely, I was smarter than this. Obviously not because here I was. I went into a very deep downward spiral emotionally. I was faced with yet another very tough decision to make. I had no idea what to do. And I knew I would not be able to count on him for much morale support considering how he now felt toward me. And I was right! He would eventually turn his back on me—just as he had done to one of his ex-girlfriends.

Something he told me about her when we first started dating came back to my remembrance. What I began to realize is that this was a pattern for him. He told me that an ex-girlfriend had become pregnant and had an abortion. When I asked him why, he said it was her choice. He said he would have married her had she decided to have it, but she aborted it because she didn't think he wanted the child. He said he never told her he did not want it nor did he tell her he did. This was now the case with us. He was such a manipulative person. I could see that now—I was dealing with a real narcissist. I was starting to see what everyone was talking about. And although I still loved him, I now saw him clearly—crystal.

Although he would never come out and say he didn't want the baby, he made it very clear to me through his actions that he did not. We would meet several times to discuss the possibilities of having a baby together; however, the entire dynamic of our relationship had changed. We would make every attempt to be cordial with one another during these times, but emotions were still very high. For all intents and purposes, he had become a stranger to me. He was a man I vaguely recognized anymore. By this time, he had grown completely comfortable saying that he was going through a selfish stage in his life. That was his go-to phrase. So now when he would act as though he was concerned for me or like he had my best interest at heart, I could see it for what it was—manipulation. His concerns extended no further than himself. He was bitter, unforgiving, and plain evil! He could no longer hide that part of himself from me.

I should have prayed and asked God to reveal to me what to do; however, I did not. God presented yet one more opportunity for me to come to him—but I didn't. I would handle this one myself—my way. I cried myself to sleep for a week. I felt myself revisiting that place I never wanted to visit again—depression. I was determined that I was not going back there no matter what. I started to weigh the costs of being a forty-one-year-old, pregnant, single, professional, and so-called saved woman. I knew there was very little hope of us ever marrying or even being together anymore. The fact of the matter was that I was starting to feel as though I couldn't possibly care less one way or the other.

As much as I still loved this man, I could not see a future with him anymore nor could I see myself having his child, so I decided the only thing I could do was to terminate the pregnancy. My closest girlfriend would take me to have the procedure done. As we sat there in the lobby waiting for my turn to terminate yet another pregnancy, I laid my head on her shoulders and just began to weep. I never saw my life being *this*. I was truly starting to question who I was. I had become someone completely different trying to love this man. I had become a stranger to my own self.

Blu continued to phone me that entire day, but I never answered. He left messages stating that he wanted to be there for me. He thought it should have been him I chose to accompany me through this process. Funny how he *now* wanted to be there for me. Now—that I'm aborting—now that he feels he's off the hook. Now he wants to be there for me? *What an asshole*, I thought. I saw it as nothing more than this being his way of ensuring the procedure went through as planned without any snafus. There was certainly no concern for me—not any more.

After many attempts to reach me, my girlfriend finally answered my phone. She told him to put the money for the procedure in my account as agreed and just leave me alone. He attempted to plead his case to her, but she was neither interested nor willing to allow him to consume anymore of our time. So he ended up doing just as she requested. He listened to her because his affiliation with her local celebrity status was good for his image. It was important to him that he not rub people like her the wrong way and that he maintained his untarnished image. And to be honest, she did not necessarily dislike him…just us being together at this point. She, along with everyone else, had come to realize that ours was just not a healthy relationship.

The very next day, after having had the procedure, I experienced a grief like never before. I was actually grieving the loss of a child—my child. This was such an excruciating pain. It hurt my very soul. I began to pray and ask God to please take the pain away. I felt like I was losing it. Satan had me just where he wanted me once again. I was defenseless or at least I felt as though I was. The more I prayed, the more I hurt. I knew that God was both disappointed in and angry with me. I felt it. I had not felt a pain like this since losing my brother in 1997. My soul was on fire. The pain was intolerable.

I thought that maybe if I talked to Blu about it, he could make me feel a little better. He was the logical thinker in our relationship, and I was the emotional one. I called him on his cell, but he would not answer. I left him messages, but he would not respond. Finally I called him at work which I had very seldom ever done over the course of our relationship. He answered and treated me as though I was a worrisome bill collector. "Tisa, what is it you need? I'm at work!" "Blu, will you please come and see me? I feel so bad right now. I just need you here with me to help me through this. Please!" I was begging and pleading with him to help me. And this was a first for me. I had never begged a man for anything—ever! My relationship with him revealed many firsts for me though. "I can't do this right now, Tisa." He hung up on me and never called back. He discarded me like I was last week's trash. I can't begin to articulate how that made me feel. I felt like next to nothing. I laid there in a ball just weeping uncontrollably.

A dear girlfriend came over to sit with me. I shared with her what had transpired, and she was in total disbelief. She held me in her arms and just rocked me for what seemed to be hours. She cried harder than I did. Although her husband and Blu were very close friends, tailgating partners and fellow Falcons' fans, she started feeling hate for him over how he was treating me. She couldn't believe how he had so easily dismissed me and my feelings during this time. But he did—and seemingly with ease. She was there for me even though I knew she was hurting inside not only for me but for her situation as well. She had always wanted a child; however, her husband selfishly changed his mind about having children after they married. He deprived her of the most precious experience she could ever have because he was too selfish to think of anyone other than himself. We were both going through. We were both grieving the absence of our babies at that time. I truly regretted this decision—more than any other poor one I had ever made.

As time went on, I began to pull myself back together, and I started to feel hatred toward Blu. I wanted to hurt him badly. I wanted him to feel what I had been feeling. I knew I was in a dangerous frame of mind, so I began to pray harder than I had in a while. And over the next month or so, my feelings of anger subsided. I didn't like him anymore, but I knew he wasn't worth me carrying such anger inside. I no longer wanted to hurt him, but I certainly would not have discouraged anyone else from doing so if they so chose.

A few months after this debacle, my closest girlfriend made the decision to return back to the radio station where she had worked for many years prior. This was wonderful news and certainly warranted a celebration. The station was throwing her a big welcome back bash at a local club in Atlanta. She invited her closest circle of friends to join her in the VIP section of the club. We were having a ball just enjoying the good company. To my utter surprise, someone approached me midways through the party and told me Blu was there. I had not seen or talked to him since the day he hung up on me—the day after I aborted our child. There were so many mixed emotions I began to feel at that moment. I couldn't believe he had the nerve to even show up. He very well knew I would be there. Why would he put us in such an awkward position? I would soon discover his plan—and it was not a good one for me. He would seek to get his revenge that night, and in many ways, he did just that.

He actually made his way into her VIP section with the rest of us. I could not believe he was that bold. He worked the crowd just as if he had actually been invited. The only reason he had gained access to that circle of friends was because of his relationship with me—which was over. *How dare he be so presumptuous to assume it was acceptable for him to be in our space? How arrogant of him*, I thought.

I looked at him as he mingled with everyone in the area, and I thought about how he had treated me only a few months back. I started to get heated. He made it a point to actually approach and mingle with just about everyone in that section. Everyone, that is, except me. He never even acknowledged my existence. You would have honestly thought that we were two strangers who had never met. This was hard for me to take. But then again, he knew it would be. There were still so many unresolved feelings. I was still extremely emotional over him, and he very well knew it.

The final straw for me was when I looked up and saw him flirting with another lady at the VIP bar. He was buying her drinks and exchanging numbers as though I wasn't even there. I witnessed him laughing and socializing with her just as he used to do with me. I knew he was bitter, but this was just a bit much for me to handle. The blatant disrespect and disregard for my feelings was unbelievable. So what did I do? Well, quite naturally, I did exactly what he knew I would do. I was nothing more than a puppet on his string. He was manipulating every move I made without as much as a word spoken directly to me.

I proceeded to the bar and intentionally positioned myself directly in between them. I asked him why he was there, and he just looked at me with a half smile on his face. I told him he needed to leave the VIP section because he had not been invited. He replied with a resounding "Fuck you. I'm not going anywhere!"

All I saw was *red* at that point. I had just spent four years of my life with this guy and just aborted a child more so for him than for myself. And he feels justified talking to me like that? The glass of wine I had in my hand ended up all over his face. He yelled "What the fuck? I can't believe you would do this!"

My friends and I left the club that night, and I had no more contact with him after that evening. It was not until the next year when my daughter was pulled over for speeding that I discovered he had actually pressed charges against me that night. That's right—he pressed charges against me for throwing a drink in his face. I fell right into his grips. He came in that night with an agenda, and I fell for it. He knew the reaction he would receive from me if he did what he did. He knew because that's just what we did. He knew, at that time, that I was broken—no different than he had been broken over us in the past. That's what we did. We broke each other. He wanted to pay me back...and he did. He made sure I was arrested and humiliated beyond belief.

I was so ashamed. I could not believe he would do something like this to me. I knew I was wrong. I was able to own that. I did *not* know that my action was considered simple assault. Had I known perhaps I would have responded differently. Then again, maybe not—I just don't know. Although the misdemeanor charge against me was dismissed and completely expunged from my record, he succeeded in accomplishing exactly what he aimed to that night. He made sure I was humiliated and shame was brought to my name. I thought about the few times I could have and even should have had him arrested for assaulting me; however, my love for him prevented me from doing so. How would he provide for his daughter were he in jail? And as much as I wanted to hate him, I couldn't. I considered contacting his employer to inform them of his illegal indiscretions he had shared with me. I thought about repaying him with evil, but I couldn't. I just kept hearing "See that none render evil for evil unto any man; but ever follow that which is good, both among yourselves, and to all men."- (1 Thessalonians 5:15) Now, more than ever, I had to allow God to handle this one, and I had to allow Him to heal my broken heart. I just had to trust Him—and I did.

Because I was obedient enough to listen to the Holy Spirit, I was avenged. I discovered that a short period after my debacle, Blu was arrested for another DUI, placed on house arrest and had to actually spend weekends in jail. I'm not saying this to bask in his misfortune. To the contrary, I only felt sorry for him when I learned of it. I say it only to serve as a reminder of how God will do just what He promises He will do to avenge you...if we'll simply allow Him. "To me belongeth vengeance, and recompence; their foot shall slide in due time: for the day of their calamity is at hand, and the things that shall come upon them make haste.- Deuteronomy 32:35

Months went by, and for the first time, neither of us reached out to the other. Although I still loved him, I knew he was toxic for me in every way. We were toxic for each other. I looked forward to the day when I could say I was completely over him. And something told me he felt the same about me. We were both good but apart from each other—certainly not together. The truth of the matter is that it would take me many years to get over him—even through years of me dating another. My truth in this matter is that I have never loved a man with the intensity I did him nor do I ever desire to again. I gave him access to a place within me where only God should dwell. Epic fail and lesson learned!

For years, I spent countless nights crying over the fact that this picture was in circulation. I sincerely felt that it was a very poor representation of the person I was—my true character. I spent thousands of dollars in attempts to have it removed from Google; however, it kept reappearing. This was my very greatest humiliation, and it served the purpose it was designed to serve. Posting this photo frees me from the guilt and shame I've always felt over it.

I'm no longer ashamed or even embarrassed by it. Instead, I allow it to serve as a reminder of the person I no longer am. "God is able to do exceedingly and abundantly above all we can ask or even think, according to the power that worketh in us" (Ephesians 3:20).

Chapter 4

The Main Chick

I dated a guy or two after the split, but no one had the ability to hold my attention for any significant period of time. Even my close girlfriends would ridicule me for being too picky. They recognized that the smallest of insignificant things in a man had a way of turning me off—for good. I looked for reasons *not* to go on a second date, and usually, I had decided this after the first ten minutes of being on the first one. I can honestly acknowledge meeting some wonderful men; but the timing obviously was not right, so nothing ever came of the encounters.

A couple of years after my break from Blu, I received a call from my closest cousin back in Tennessee. He told me he was out and about and had someone with him who wanted to meet me. He then told me the guy was a former NFL player. I was instantly opposed to the idea of meeting him. Being a former athlete myself and often accused of having unhealthy levels of testosterone in my DNA, I was hip to their games. I was not interested in being with anyone who could possibly be a player not to mention someone who thought they were finer than me. I had dated athletes my entire life, but this time, I was hesitant because I knew what came along with it. I was not about to compete for a man—not at this point in my life.

I began to ask my cousin a series of questions. "How does this guy know of me?" "What kind of person is he?" My cousin assured me that he was a good guy. Although they did not know each other well, he was someone my cousin thought I would get along well with. He told me that BJ seemed very low-key, soft spoken, and not at all argumentative. That was music to my ears. I instructed my cousin *not* to give him my phone number. I told him to advise the guy to look me up on Facebook. And he did just that—immediately.

I could say that this guy was certainly easy on the eyes. In fact, he was a vision of loveliness. Extremely fit, well groomed, and *chocolate*! From a physical perspective, he was one of the most handsome men I'd ever seen…which was a real concern to me. Why was he single? How long has he been single? How many hearts has he broken in his lifetime? He's in Tennessee, so why in the world would he desire to date someone in Georgia? I had a ton of doubts and even more reason why I wouldn't be interested in him. But because my cousin, whom I trusted with my life, saw something in him, I said I would at least talk to him. My cousin knew me better than probably any other man alive. If he co-signed, it probably couldn't hurt to meet him.

After several hours of texting that night, he asked if I would be comfortable talking to him. To this point, I was slightly impressed with his answers to all my questions, so I allowed the conversation to take place. I was not at all optimistic, though. I knew he would say something to turn me off during the course of our conversation. Surprisingly, he didn't. He was extremely transparent and forthcoming. Even though some of the things he said gave me pause, it wasn't enough to keep me from cautiously moving forward. He told me he had grown accustomed to having a main chick and a side chick but that he had no desire to continue that path. He said it was too emotionally exhausting and that he really had a desire to do right by God. This caught my attention because I had been praying for a godly man. My response to him was very direct.

"I'm not interested in being anybody's side chick or even their main chick. If I'm not the *only* chick, I don't want any parts of it."

We began an instant courtship. Even though I had taken very little interest in anyone since Blu, there was something about this man that I liked. He was soothing to my soul. Our conversations came very easily—no dead silence. We would talk for two to three hours every night. His voice would become the first one I heard each morning and the last one every night. He wooed me with beautiful quotes he would text me every day.

"I wanna be the reason why you smile today."

"Today I started smiling for no apparent reason. Then I realized I was thinking of you."

"Every time you think of me today, just know I'll be thinking of you at the very same time."

Little quotes like these put a smile on my face and really aided in ridding me of any inhibitions I may have had at that time. He was sensitive, attentive, and just what I felt I needed in my life. I had begun to wonder if I would ever be able to fall in love with another man after Blu, and it didn't look good—until now. So naturally, when it was time for us to actually meet in person, I was extremely nervous. A huge part of me expected that I would find a reason to be turned off by him. I remember my best friend, Kelly, jokingly praying to God that BJ would do nothing to turn me off.

"God, please don't let this man walk up in here chewing gum and smiling at the same time."

"And, God, please don't let this man have dirty shoestrings or a corny smile."

We laughed our heads off, but secretly, I was praying similar prayers myself.

He came to my job for our first in-person meeting. From the word hello, I absolutely knew that this was a man I wanted to get to know better. I was definitely interested in this one. And for the first time in over two years, I found myself feeling excited about the possibilities. He gave me no reason to push my pause button. We spent the weekend together, and what a weekend it was. We hang out with friends, shooting pool, dancing, and just enjoying each other's company. He quickly fit right in to the circle of friends that surrounded me. There was nothing to this point that I didn't like about this man.

He had a youthful quality about him—almost little boyish. He was always seeking to learn from others. Like a sponge, he soaked up all the knowledge he could get from anyone. He also had a real interest in knowing how the men in my life treated me prior to him. It was as though he wanted to immolate their good qualities because he lacked confidence in his own. Although I was not comfortable discussing my past relationships, he had no problem pulling information about me, my family, and my past relationships from a plethora of people. This bothered me a bit because he would never reveal his sources. But I supposed he was well within his rights to do so. This was just something I had never experienced.

We couldn't seem to get enough of each other in the beginning. Although he lived in Tennessee where I was from, his roots were deeply planted here in Georgia. It was rather ironic in that he was living in my hometown, and I was residing in his. I was accustomed to my past relationships becoming serious rather quickly, and this one was no different. I wasn't crazy about the distance, but he made up for it by coming to see me very regularly. His job afforded him the luxury of having one complete week off during the month plus an additional long weekend. Needless to say, he divided that time between me and his family.

I had never met a family quite like his. They found a way to turn just about any occasion into a reason to party. And they partied hard. They thoroughly enjoyed each other's company when they weren't fighting—literally. BJ would have pretty regular bouts with his siblings and mother. They fought hard but loved even harder. It took me no time to see that I was embarking upon even more dysfunction than I had been accustomed to. By this time, I loved him and convinced myself that I had no right to judge them just because they were different from my family. I mean, let's face it—we were far from perfect, so who was I to judge?

Although we really enjoyed each other's company and had crazy chemistry for each other, our relationship was anything but perfect. BJ was very predictable. He did things the same way every time—like the phone calls in the mornings, afternoons, and evening. So when things weren't as I expected them to be, it gave me pause and made me raise one eyebrow. The first time we experienced turbulence in our relationship was several months after we started seeing each other. It was the weekend of his alma mater's homecoming at the University of Tennessee. After growing used to speaking with him like clockwork every day, he mysteriously vanished for that entire weekend.

Like many women, I have been blessed with that sixth sense. I started to feel sick at my stomach—I knew something wasn't right. I had already surmised that he was probably entertaining someone from his past—or perhaps even his present. I figured he would call me when she left on that Sunday with some lame excuse. I was right. Just as I had expected, he called me late Sunday afternoon after having not called or taken my calls since Friday. I wasn't the least bit interested in what he had to say, so I didn't answer the phone that entire day nor did I answer it the next day or the day after that. He went from leaving very calm voice messages explaining his disappearance to leaving very angry messages telling me he didn't need me!

"Okay, Tisa. So I see you're just not gonna take my call. It's cool. I was good before you, and I damn sure will be good after you!"

As far as I was concerned, the relationship was over. I should have paid closer attention to the details in our initial conversation. I was a little upset by it all because I had grown to love him; however, I was not at all emotionally distraught. If I learned nothing else from my previous relationship, I learned to always guard my heart. I was determined to *never* allow a man the same access to me that I gave Blu.

Sure, I would miss the awesome sex—especially the new stunts he exposed me to. He was a very muscular guy, so he just showed out during our sexual encounters. He was the first man to ever treat my body like dumbbells he was curling in the gym during sex. And he was certainly the first one to ever lift and straddle me over his shoulders while taking care of me. But, although different, I'd already had better sex with Blu, so I figured it was nothing I couldn't do without.

I needed to know that I could love another man after Blu. There was a part of me that felt like I would never be able to love again—and a bigger part that didn't even know if I wanted to. One thing was for certain—I had no desire to love that same way again. And I didn't. But it gave me solace just to know that I actually had the capacity in my heart to love someone else. It gave me hope in an otherwise hopeless situation. Even if I had to wait another two years, I was content with doing so because I knew that eventually, it would happen for me again.

Several weeks went by, and he was prompted to reach out to me again. This time, I actually answered my phone. I don't know why, except that I missed him. I was good at being stubborn. I actually had mastered it. He began to tell me about the weekend in question. He swore that he had not cheated on me. He said he and some fellow college athlete buddies had gotten a hotel and stayed drunk the entire weekend. Of course, I didn't believe him, but I entertained his conversation. I mean, I felt it was probably the least I could do since he had obviously exhausted so many brain cells coming up with such a creative story.

BJ was an intelligent guy, but he often struggled with ways to effectively express that intellect verbally. He was a big boy from the country and had often been ridiculed and teased because of his dialect. Admittedly, I had been guilty of teasing him a time or two myself. It was all in fun. And fortunately, he had enough of a sense of humor to see it for what it was. I was never bothered by the fact that he talked differently from me or my friends. On the contrary, I learned to embrace it.

I remember one of my girlfriends asking me a pretty tough question about him, though.

"T, I can admit that BJ is some serious eye candy, and he may even be the bomb in bed; however, what are you gonna do when that part of the relationship gets old?"

"Girl, you know good and well you are *strongly* drawn to intellect. This nigga can't match wits with you, nor will he be able to stimulate you intellectually on *any* level for *any* period of time. I'm just saying." That was a little hard to hear, especially now that I really cared for him. But the fact of the matter was, she was right. So I was speechless—totally speechless.

I finally spoke up in his defense and told her that this guy really is more intelligent than he appears to be. I backed it up by telling her that he had read the Bible, in its entirety, not once but twice.

"Can you say you've ever accomplished that?" I asked her.

Her very sarcastic reply was, "He may have read it, but did he understand it?"

Again, she rendered me speechless. I knew that there was some truth to what she was saying. But, for the moment, I was okay with him being Mr. "Right Now" instead of Mr. "Right." I was going to enjoy just living for the moment. This was advice I decided to take from my girl, Kelly, who always accused me of overthinking things too much. "T, I'm gonna need you to be ok with just living for the moment sometimes! No pressure, no expectations. Just enjoy the journey."

I forgave him for whatever actually happened the weekend of his homecoming, and we picked up where we left off. I will say, though, that I became aware. My heart was guarded now more than ever before. I also started to keep my options open—at least to some degree. I thought that if I, at least, continued to communicate with other men, it would keep me from getting too caught up in him. In many ways, I was right. But it didn't come without its fair share of problems.

I think I fell in love with BJ, but I can't be completely certain. There were times when I felt complete with him—happy and ful-filled. I never, though, felt like I couldn't live without him. And often times, I was as happy to see him leave as I was to see him come—especially when there had been any confusion between us during his visit. We were on and off from the very beginning, so perhaps my expectations of the relationship were just not as high as they had been of other serious ones in the past. We were very different individuals with very different morals and values. I'm not saying mine were bet-ter than his or vice versa, just different.

There was a big part of him that was extremely immature. Now topple that with the fact that he was a bit of a player and the absolute *most*-argumentative and easily-offended man I had ever met in my life. It just didn't always make for a quality relationship. He appealed to me in other ways, though. Most of which were very physical in nature. BJ was very attractive, and he took great pride in keeping his body together and remaining extremely fit. He had many female fans—their thirst was very real, and they could not care less that he was dating me. To look at him, you would think he had it all together. You would assume he was the most confident man in the world. But the closer we grew and the deeper he started to care for me, the more insecure he became.

We both experienced spurts of feeling insecure when it came to our relationship. It often made things much more difficult than they should have had to be. We both had our different hang ups, but they were very real and justified to us. I experienced feelings of insecurity due to what seemed to be his inability to stop communicating with other women. His stemmed from the knowledge that he could never live up to my exes. He always felt like I secretly compared him to them. Perhaps I did, to a certain degree. I knew, though, that he could not offer me what they had; however, I really could appreciate his effort for the most part. He wanted to do better. He wanted to be better, and I recognized that in him. Unfortunately, it could not overcompensate for the demons he battled.

One night, we were at some friends' home. By this time, we had been seeing each other for well over two years. We were having a wonderful evening just enjoying good food, drinks, and company. He gave me his phone to look at something. While I was doing so, he received a text message. And, yes, I read it. It stated, "I see you're still playing games, BJ." I can't really explain the feeling that I had. It was rather nonchalant. I was not greatly affected by it at all. I almost expected him to receive a message like this. I returned his phone to him and very inconspicuously said, "You may wanna check your messages." He began explaining something I was not the least bit interested in hearing. So as he began telling me that this was an old fat lady who liked him but no one he had an interest in, I just shut the conversation down. I didn't feel it was the time or place as others were around. "BJ, I'm really not interested in having this conversation right now. We can talk about this later if you feel the need to do so." I can honestly say that I was not loud or rude in my delivery to him, but for some reason, this absolutely infuriated him. He got up from his chair and pushed me in my chest with all his force. I was completely caught off guard by this. In a million years, I never saw this one coming. I knew he had his issues; however, I never had him pegged to be a violent man towards women. He had never shown me any signs of it.

I couldn't help but remember all the stories I had heard about how he would mutilate his brother when they would fight. I thought that was just a sibling rivalry. Never did I expect to be on the receiving end of his bullying and violence. He also shared with me that his father was a violent man. He used to abuse their mother and eventually began abusing BJ and his younger brother. This was when his mother made the decision to leave him. What was I doing to continuously attract these violent men? I knew I could be mouthy at times, and I acknowledged this character flaw within myself. The fact of the matter, though, was that they were violent prior to ever meeting me. They suppressed it well, but there was still something in me that attracted these types of men to me. What was it? What vibe was I giving off?

After I had a second to process what had just happened, I very calmly got out of my seat, walked inside to the kitchen area where my friend's family members were gathered around the table playing cards. I cordially spoke to them all, even to the extent of exchanging smiles and casual conversation. "Y'all doing ok in here?" I asked. They were totally unaware of what had just transpired a few feet away from them on the other side of the door. I opened one of the kitchen drawers and proceeded to grab the largest butcher knife I could find, smiled at them once again and went back out the same door I entered in through. I had snapped—completely! I planned on gutting him like a fish—literally. I always knew I had a very violent side to me, but I tried to avoid being in the presence of others who brought it out of me. As I attempted to get to him, our friends got in between us, allowing him free passage to leave.

After he left, we all sat there in disbelief over what had just transpired. No one saw that coming. It literally came from nowhere. BJ began to call after only a few minutes of being gone. When I didn't answer, he called each friend over and over until one of them finally answered his call. He was extremely apologetic and could not believe what he had done. He begged us to allow him to come back, so he could talk to me. I wouldn't even consider it. Our friends urged him to give me some time. They told him he was not welcome back there that night. I knew that would be the last time I ever spoke with him. I was in shock!

Several weeks passed, and he was beginning to wear me down. I was really missing him and wanted to hear what he had to say about why he reacted that way. So eventually, I listened. I knew I would regret it later because I was aware of where it would lead. We would end up back together and ultimately become the talk of our circle. I had completely lost myself and obviously any self-worth while trying to maintain this and the last relationship. And although my feelings for BJ were not nearly as strong as they had been for Blu, he had become very familiar to me. I was completely comfortable around him, just being myself—flaws, and all. He accepted me just as I was. That's not to say he would miss an opportunity to argue about something I had done or said at the drop of a dime. I don't think he would have had it any other way, actually.

After our conversation, I spoke to the couple whose home we were at when the altercation ensued. BJ had been communicating with them the entire time I wasn't speaking to him. They convinced me that I should consider giving him another chance. I think they missed him being around as much as I did, so their advice was probably selfishly given. They shared with me an incident where something similar had happened in their marriage—he pushed her. They justified his actions by saying that he, at least, did not hit me. I listened, and it made sense to me. Perhaps it was because they were saying what I wanted to hear at just that moment. At any rate, it comforted me. And I eventually welcomed him back into my life.

Perhaps my greatest concern with BJ was the fact that my baby girl never truly warmed up to him. I didn't understand because they never saw us argue nor was there ever any confusion displayed in their presence. I asked her one day to just tell me what it was about him she did not like. I knew that if I ever had to choose between him and my girls, he was history—for *real*. I will never forget her answer at only thirteen years old.

She said, "Mommy, it's not that I don't like him. I just don't like him for you."

I persisted, "Baby, has he ever said or done anything to you that made you uncomfortable?"

She insisted that he had not. She just felt he was not *my type*. She also did not think he had the capacity to really connect with her as my child. She would say, "I'm the kid. He should connect with me—not the other way around."

Although I knew she was right, the fact that he had never done or said anything out of the way to them gave me a little peace about remaining with him. He had his own two boys that he never really connected with, so why in the world would I expect that he would be able to connect with mine? Why? Because Blu did. But then again, he wasn't Blu. And he often reminded me of that.

I remember several occasions when BJ would blatantly ask me, "Tisa, why am I here? What is it you want from me? I can't be your exes, so why do you even want me? Why do you love me?"

As well as I was able to articulate my feelings in most cases, I truly struggled conjuring up an answer to these questions. It rendered me speechless. I knew I could fix him if he would just allow me to do so. I could mold him into the perfect man for me if he would just submit and allow me to do so. I could make him a better man. I could have that man who completed that *power couple* image that I once had with my husband. I think that's why I stayed so long. I remained with him though some of my girlfriends would tell me that he was bringing me down socially. They would tell me he just wasn't on my level, and I was settling. It was hard to hear, but I knew they were probably right.

BJ accompanied me to a few of my company's holiday parties. He was the life of the party, typically, and kept everyone in stitches. However, at one particular party, there was tension between us, and his actions, again, were inexcusable. We were staying the night at the host hotel in Buckhead. He was several libations in by the time we arrived downstairs for the festivities. As the night progressed, he became more and more convinced that my Vice President wanted me for himself. Topple his feelings of insecurity with the fact that I had rejected his request to dance the last time he asked, and this was a recipe for complete disaster. He began yelling at me, "Tisa, if that short, black motherfucker gets in your face one more time, I'm gonna kill him tonight!" I tried my best to calm him down, but he was clearly at a point of absolutely no return. "You can't dance with me cause your feet hurt, but you can turn on the smiles for him all night long? Get the fuck outta here!"

I tried reassuring him in an effort to settle him down. I pointed out the fact that my VP was there with his wife and had no desire to be with me. I even offered to dance again at that point, even though my feet were killing me. Nothing was working. He wanted to stay mad…and he did. I started to feel myself becoming more and more agitated. I was embarrassed and a bit humiliated. I felt as though everyone was looking directly at us. "BJ, if you do anything to further humiliate me in the presence of my superiors and direct reports, I will never forgive you." He didn't care at that point. He was growing more and more belligerent every minute that passed. Finally, my best friend's husband along with another friend had to take him out of the party all together. There was no reasoning with him at all.

All three couples gathered in our hotel room shortly thereafter. Everyone wanted to see the tension subside, so we could all just enjoy the rest of the night. BJ was fine and seemed to be back to his normal jolly and playful self while everyone was there. The guys were riding him pretty hard about how he had acted. It was a joke to them. They were all amused. However, as soon as they left, he quickly wanted to revisit the argument we were having at the party. I begged him to just allow me to go to sleep and I encouraged him to do the same. "BJ, if you'll just let me go to sleep, I'll answer any questions you have in the morning…I promise!" My hope was that he would sleep the alcohol off and realize how ridiculous his actions were the entire night. "Hell no, Tisa! We gonna talk about this shit right now!" I begged him to keep his voice down, as I had no way of knowing who was in the rooms next to us. It could have been the very executive in question, himself. He was totally out of control, to the point of pulling all the covers off of me, so I couldn't ignore him. This went on until approximately 5:00 am. By then, he had tired himself out and felt he needed some rest, I suppose. I guess he eventually got tired of arguing by his self, because I had completely shut down hours prior to this.

Incidents like this one were very common with BJ. He was a big guy and he flaunted his massive muscles and strength when he needed to. I spent countless nights up, just listening to him throw temper tantrums, all in the name of love. He truly felt it was what needed to be done to get to the bottom of any issues we may have had, when all I wanted to do was just sleep. I knew there was no talking to him when he was angry, so I wouldn't even attempt to. But he would not be ignored…please make no mistake about that! By the time the morning would come, I would be so over him until I could hardly wait to be as far away from him as I could possibly get. I can remember telling him on numerous occasions "If I lived close to the Empire State Building, I promise I would climb every step, and jump off, just to get away from you right now!" He had a way of interrogating me to near death.

In addition to everything else that seemed to be going wrong in our relationship, BJ's interactions with Calvin really began to concern me—greatly! They were formally introduced toward the beginning of our relationship. They spoke and shook hands. That would be the last and only conversation they would ever have. They would literally be in the very same room within a few feet of one another but would not acknowledge each other in any way. The tension was thick enough to cut with a knife.

BJ always felt that Calvin wanted me back. His main reason was because Cal would hand-deliver the child support payments instead of depositing them into my account. He felt as though Calvin would use any excuse he could come up with to drop by my home—and he was not comfortable with that, so I stopped it. But the damage was already done. I really started to fear that something bad was going to transpire between the two of them. Although Calvin was a relatively mild-mannered person, BJ was not. And they were both capable of producing massive collateral damage. It was just becoming too hard with BJ in every way.

The very last tumultuous incident between us sealed our fate. He hurt his shoulder lifting weights and had to have surgery to correct it. I went to Tennessee to be there with him during his operation. I had even gone out the day before the surgery and purchased things for his apartment to make it more warm and inviting for him after he was released from the hospital. I surprised him by fixing up both bathrooms with pictures, candles, rugs, and other little trinkets, while he was at work. I wanted him to be completely relaxed and pleased while he was home resting, as he was very depressed over the fact that he could not lift weights for six months. He seemed to be very grateful for the things I had done and loved the look I had created for him.

A few days after the surgery, we made the decision that he would come back to Georgia and stay with me so I could help him throughout this healing process. He needed someone with him because he had no use of his right arm. Although I had to work, I would drop in on him from time to time to see how he was doing. One day, within the first week of him being there, I came home unexpectedly. As soon as I got there, his phone rang, but he did not answer it. "Why aren't you answering your phone, BJ?" I asked. "I don't recognize the number." He insisted. I knew he was lying and this infuriated me! I mean, after all, here I am taking care of this guy and he's up to no good??? And in MY home??? Who does that??? I saw this as blatant disrespect and I wasn't having it!

Needless to say, an argument ensued. "Call the number back, BJ. Let's see who it is." He adamantly refused. He had no intentions of allowing me to know who she was. I went outside because I felt myself getting heated…really heated. A few minutes later, he came out and handed me his phone, in an effort to ease my mind. I searched to call log and the number was no longer there. This guy had actually gone through and erased every number he didn't want me to see. How did I know this, you ask? Because the only remaining numbers in his phone were those of mine and his mother's. Did he really think I would fall for that??? The words that would proceed from my mouth next were a true testament to how sharp my tongue could be when I got angry. "You big, dumb, backwoods, slave-ass, country nigga, who can't make your subject and verb matter agree to save your life! You have the nerve to insult MY intelligence? Are you kidding me? Who the hell do you take me for?

I told him to get all his shit together and get out of my home! He was no longer welcome. It became a real shouting match at that point. We both called each other some real choice names that cut us to the core. I took him to the corner gas station and threw him and his luggage out on the curb, where a family member later picked him up. This was it for us and our love affair. I felt completely disrespected and unappreciated, while he felt as though I kicked him while he was down. Both may have been true, but it was totally irrelevant at that point.

Our relationship lasted almost five years with more time apart than together. I found myself conforming to his lifestyle more so than he was conforming to mine. He came from a family that loved to drink and party—a lot. I was drifting farther and farther away from God. I didn't seem to be able to find my way back. And to be honest, I really wasn't trying that hard to. Our relationship was plagued with extreme jealousy on both sides, arguments, and outside influences. At day end, it just became too hard to deal with. We both began to lose interest and long for something easier. He would always say he could tell I had other men in my ear because of how nonchalant I had become. And he was right—I did. Although we had a great deal of love for one another, the breakup was easy—painless. It was just time. We ended things and went our separate ways. We would still communicate and even get together from time to time, but those strong feelings for one another that we had once possessed were no longer there. It was truly over.

Chapter 5

Spiritual Warfare

I began to experience some really strange things after my dad passed in 2011. I remember shortly after he passed I spoke with my bishop and First Lady after a church service. They were aware of my loss and offered their condolences and a prophetic word. I have to tell you that I was somewhat concerned by what my bishop said.

He said, "You will begin to notice that much of your father's spirit will begin to manifest and show up in you."

Although my father was one of the absolute *best* fathers I had ever witnessed with regards to loving, protecting, and being present in the lives of his children, I don't ever recall him being referenced as a godly man. He was good man—a very good one, but like most of us all, he battled his demons. And they seemed to intensify after my brother's death.

It was important to my dad that he be strong for me and my baby sister after Patrick's death. He was outwardly strong for us. He was always checking up on us and offering words of encouragement to help us get through. All the while, he was dying on the inside. He and Patrick, over the years, had become best friends. My brother was a professional bodybuilder, and my dad was his biggest fan. That was "his boy" as he so often passionately referred to him. My father was so very proud of him—almost to the point of idolizing him and his accomplishments.

After Patrick died, my dad began to drink heavily in an effort to mask his pain. There were many times he would call me or my sister one night, piss us off with some off-kilter conversation, and not even remember having had the conversation the very next day. My father had always been an overprotective worrywart when it came to his three children—always! It intensified for me and my sister after Pat's death. He went from calling once a day to sometimes several times a day just to make sure we were okay. It would drive me and my sister up the wall sometimes. We would often joke about his calls being border-line harassment. We took for granted that he would always be here. We never imagined that he too would be taken from us prematurely. He would certainly outlive us all, we thought. But he would end up dying in a car accident that eerily mirrored that of my brother's. He died from the same massive head trauma injury.

After my dad's death, things started happening in my home that were hard to explain. The standing joke between my girls would become that we had a ghost in our house. My baby girl even named him Bob. They had many counts of doors shutting by themselves, strange noises, and other weird things happening when I was away from the house. I honestly just discounted them all. I never imagined that they could be anything more than their vivid imaginations or mere coincidences. I thought that the house was settling and moving as many homes do. That would always be my explanation to them.

There were many times I would notice that when I was alone in the home and in bed, I would smell a foul odor. It smelled like flatulence. I would get up to make sure the gas was off on the stove…and it always was. I would find nothing out of the ordinary. I couldn't figure out where the odor was coming from because I would be the only one in the home. I would just discount it, turn over, and go back to sleep.

When Jhordyn was entering high school, I sold that home and moved to a county that had a better school system. I downsized slightly, but I was so excited and looking forward to our new beginnings in our new space. It was in a much more rural environment than what we were used to, and Jhordyn absolutely despised it. She and Jazmen would always say that I moved them out in the middle of nowhere. But it was important to me that my baby be in an environment where she could flourish and grow academically and socially. I also wanted to expose them to much more diversity as my youngest really struggled with her perception of white people. It was her opinion that they were all like the corrupt police officers she would read about daily who were killing innocent black people. I explained to her that her stereotyping them was in fact no different than what she hated most about them. If I could expose her to just *one* decent one, I felt I would be doing her a service. And that's exactly what happened.

A few months after being in Fayetteville, I remember Jhordyn calling me at work. She was terrified. She said, "Mommy, someone is in the house with me. I just heard Jazmen's door slam."

Jaz's room was right beside her room. I was far away from her and concerned, but I was also hoping she was being overly dramatic as I thought she was in our last home. It was almost like the little boy who cried wolf at this point. I told her to answer the phone as I FaceTimed her. I also told her to pick up a heavy object in her bedroom to use as a weapon if necessary. I walked her through each and every possible space in the home. She opened every closet door and looked under every bed—but there was nothing. I left work and came home to be with her anyway because I could tell she was extremely shaken. I kept her on the phone the entire drive home.

A few months later, on a Sunday afternoon, she wanted me to watch a scary movie with her. I usually wouldn't agree to do this; however, I gave in to her pleas this day. The movie was called *The Conjuring*. There was one particular scene in the movie that captured my attention. It was the part where the one child kept accusing the other one of passing gas. Although the other swore they did not do it, the odor was present. This made me think of all the times this had happened to me both in the old home and now in the new one. I googled *foul gas odors* after we watched the movie. What I discovered blew me away. Many historians and religious figures considered this to be the presence of a dark or satanic spirit. Could this possibly be happening to me? Could my girls have been telling the truth all along? How could this be? I had never experienced anything of the sort; however, I absolutely could not deny the fact that it made perfect sense.

Although I didn't want to believe this could be the case, I became aware. And that's when things started to get real. I was now aware and no longer discounting crazy, inexplicable incidents that continued to happen in my home. After this point, things—very eerie things began to happen. I never would tell anyone because I didn't want them to think something was wrong with us or our home. I kept it to myself and even attempted to downplay the situation to my girls. I did not want them to be uncomfortable in their own home even though their mommy was beginning to feel that way.

It went from the foul odor to random things starting to break down around the home. For instance, within the first year in my home, I replaced everything from plumbing appliances, garage doors, to garbage disposals. You name it. I replaced it. One New Year's Eve, when BJ and I were still dating, we threw a party. A few close couples stayed the night with us. I was awakened out of my sleep the next morning because I was freezing. I went downstairs to the furnace only to discover it was 61 degrees in my home. The furnace had broken. I knew then that this was more than a coincidence. My home was only ten years old, but at the rate that things were breaking, it should have been twenty-five years or older.

A year or so after moving in, one of my close girlfriends needed to stay with me for a while as she and her husband worked on some serious marital issues. I knew she was a very godly woman, and I knew that if there was truly a presence there, she would be able to experience it. I never mentioned it to her because again, part of me was in denial, and the other part was embarrassed. I know this might sound crazy, but it's truly how I felt. Why would some demonic spirit attach itself to me or my home? I had never experienced anything of the sort nor did I truly even believe it could happen. I knew what the Bible stated about these spirits, but I was not a true believer until paranormal things began to happen in my home.

I was at work and Jhordyn was at school the first day my girlfriend came to move her things in. She stayed in Jazmen's room upstairs as Jaz was staying with her dad at the time. As soon as we got home, Ursula began telling me that something had happened when she was putting her things away in the bedroom.

She said, "Teese, I was placing my clothes in the chest upstairs. And the large heavy conch shell that sits on top of the dresser fell to the floor."

I asked her if she had inadvertently shaken the chest.

She said, "I absolutely did not. As a matter of fact, I was nowhere near it when it fell. Something pushed that shell to the floor. It was securely placed on the top of that dresser."

I asked her what happened after that, and she said she began speaking in tongues and pleading the blood of Jesus over my home. She said fear overtook her, but she was cognizant enough to call on the name of Jesus. I was blown away, but I knew what it was with absolute surety now. There was no more doubt in my mind that I had a dark spirit dwelling within my home. I can't say it was an evil one because it never seemed to want to bring us harm. Just wanted its presence to be known.

I became fearful at this point. I would pray, but it was as though my prayers were falling upon deaf ears. I knew how I had been living, and I couldn't blame God for not hearing me. Ursula and I never spoke about that incident again nor did I ever admit to having suspicions prior to her moving in. Maybe it was because I was pulling from her spiritual connection to God to help me combat any negative energy that was there. I did not want her to leave us—not now. I didn't think I could handle this thing on my own. Nothing seemed to happen when we were there together, and Ursula never mentioned anything else happening aside from that one incident.

Several months passed, and Ursula started spending more and more time at her home with her husband and family. I had become fearful of going home and being alone in the house by this time. The spirit was around me all the time when I was at home. I could feel it as strongly as I felt any other living person standing beside me. I felt as though I no longer had the relationship I needed with God to combat it. I tried to pray it away, but nothing happened. I was scared in my own home. And what was worse was that I told no one. Not my kids, friends, or family—no one knew but me. I honestly felt as though I was losing my mind.

The breaking point for me was one evening when Jhordyn called me at work and said that she could not get into the house. Her garage code was not working. It was starting to get dark outside, and I was at least thirty minutes from her. I started to feel a knot in the pit of my stomach. I knew this had something to do with the spirit in our home. Fortunately, we had a neighbor who was walking in the neighborhood. She was a kind, little white lady who was frequently seen walking around the community. She saw Jhordyn standing outside and asked if she was okay. Jhordyn told her what happened and that she was waiting for me to get home. She was kind enough to take Jhordyn around the corner a couple of miles to my sister's house, but no one was there. She allowed Jhordyn to stay at her home until I could get there. A huge weight was lifted off me because I knew my baby was safe.

I picked Jhordyn up and was relieved that she had been fed and well taken care of. I was indebted to my neighbor. And this random act of kindness allowed Jhordyn to be a witness to the fact that there were, indeed, very decent and caring white people in this world. As we pulled up to our home, it was like a scene from a scary movie. Every home on our street was fully lit, and there sat my home—in total and complete darkness. I had no power in my home which is why Jhordyn's code did not work. I was scared and mad all at the same time. I knew my electric bill was paid, so there was no logical explanation as to why my power was out. I called the power company, and they could not offer any kind of explanation. They sent someone out immediately to fix the problem. When the tech arrived, he worked for about an hour then told me something that made my heart pound heavily.

"Ms. Walker, I have no idea what has happened to your power. I've never seen anything like this." He explained that he could not get it restored and would have to call in an overnight crew to dig up all my electrical wiring underground. He was puzzled because he said that both homes on both sides of me were all powered by the very same source; so if something was wrong with the main source, their power should be out as well, but it was not. He said if something is wrong with just part of the source, we would at least have partial power; but we have none. He was puzzled, and I was terrified now!

I knew I had to say something at this point. I could not do this by myself anymore. We packed an overnight bag and went to stay at my sister's. I pulled her back in to her bedroom and broke down and told her everything that had been happening. She just started crying. She felt so bad that I had been going through it for so long and kept it to myself. Although she is my baby sister, she has always been a protector; and she was rendered helpless in this situation. She told me of some similar things that had been happening to her but nothing to the degree I was experiencing. We both wondered if this had anything to do with our father. We didn't want to believe it did, but we knew it was a strong possibility.

We agreed that it was time to call our mother and stepdad. He is a pastor, and my mom had always been very strong and deeply rooted in the Word. They began to pray and pull down strongholds. We talked for hours, and although I felt a little relief that I had prayer partners, the bulk of my relief was that I had shared it with someone. I still felt the presence when we returned home the next morning, and I began to get angry. It felt really dark, intrusive, and dominant. It felt scary and mysterious. I had never dealt with any dark spirits of this magnitude prior to this. I didn't feel as though I could. But what I did know was that I was prepared to die in my attempts to, if it meant protecting my children.

After Jhordyn went to school, I started screaming at it. I was at my wits' end. I couldn't take it anymore. "What do you want from me? Why are you here bothering us? Why won't you leave us the hell alone? I'm sick of you! This is my home and you are not welcomed here!"

My mom called me later that day and said that as she was interceding for me, my bishop's face kept coming to her. "Tisa, I know you may not feel comfortable doing so, but you need to reach out to him." she said. I had not been right with God and had just returned to the choir. I would have to be completely transparent with him and let him know I was not as strong in the Lord as he may have considered me to be. I mean, I was up ministering songs to thousands of people in our congregation. I shouldn't be dealing with this. And if I were, I should know how to plead the blood of Jesus and take my home back—but I couldn't! I was so ashamed to expose my imperfections, but I realized something had to be done. I decided to wait a few days to see if anything changed, but it didn't. I sat down and typed my bishop a message—very long message. I disclosed everything about what was happening, how I was feeling, and I reminded him of what he had prophesied to me when my dad died and how uncomfortable that made me feel. I told him I felt like I was losing it. I told him that I was truly fearful.

I wasn't sure how long it would take him to respond or if he even would. I never wanted to be a burden to my bishop or to anyone for that matter. I understood very clearly that he had over twenty thousand members to contend with. I was just a small fish in a very large pond. To my surprise and delight, he responded in no time—almost immediately. He told me that he was interceding on behalf of me and my girls. He also gave me Scripture and Verse to meditate on both day and night. It was Psalms 91, and I did just that!

He that dwelleth in the secret place of the Most High, shall abide under the shadow of the Almighty. I will say of the Lord, He is my refuge and my fortress: my God, in Him will I trust. Surely He shall deliver thee from the snare of the fowler, and from the noisome pestilence. He shall cover thee with his feathers, and under his wings shalt thou trust: His truth shall be thy shield and buckler. Thou shalt not be afraid for the terror by night; nor for the arrow that flieth by day, Nor for the pestilence that walketh in darkness; nor for the destruction that wasteth at noonday. A thousand shall fall at thy side and ten thousand at thy right hand; but it shall not come nigh thee. Only with thine eyes shalt thou behold and see the reward of the wicked. Because thou hast made the Lord, which is my refuge, even the most High, thy habitation; There shall no evil befall thee, neither shall any plague come nigh thy dwelling. For He shall give His angels charge over thee, to keep thee in all thy ways. They shall bear thee up in their hands, lest thou dash thy foot against a stone. Thou shalt tread upon the lion and the adder: the young lion and the dragon shalt thy trumple under feet. Because he hath set his love upon me, therefore will I deliver him: I will set him on high, because he hath known my name. He shall call upon me and I will answer him: I will be with him in trouble; I will deliver him, and honour him. With long life I will satisfy him, and shew him my salvation.

This Scripture and Verse became a part of me! I allowed it to completely permeate every fiber of my being. I also cleared out a closet in my bedroom and that became my *war room*. I closed myself off and prayed harder than I had ever prayed before in that room. I wrote Scriptures and Verses that I wanted to meditate on, and I read them daily. I would make my declarations from that space each day. In just a matter of weeks, I felt my strength coming back. I made a vow to the Lord that if He would see fit to tag team with me on this one, I would do my very best to do right by Him. In no time at all, I started to feel a peace in my home. My God, it felt so good. My home was clean of any dark spirits. I could feel it. I surrendered my life to Him again—completely this time. I became stronger in His Word than I ever had before.

I prayed for Him to clean me up from the inside out. I wanted—I needed to feel His presence in my life daily. Some days, I felt Him stronger than others, but I always knew He was with me. I was confident in this. Before, I always took for granted that He was always there with me and that I really owed Him nothing for it in return. Ironically, I discovered that I owed Him *everything*! I realized that I am absolutely nothing without Him in my life. I can do nothing. I can be nothing without God.

I came to realize that I didn't know the Lord as well as I thought I did. I didn't have my own personal relationship with Him. I believed in Him just because I had been told I should. Although He had always seen me through tough situations, I'm not convinced that I truly knew His power until now. I would never view Him the same. I wanted Him to be pleased with me in all I did possibly for the first time in my life. I was so very desperate for Him—for his presence. I longed to feel him always, and when I didn't, I prayed that much harder.

Now with that being said, I can't say that the enemy has not tried me from time to time. What I can say is that I handle him very differently now. I speak to him with the authority given to me by the Holy Spirit. I remember one day, after a plethora of different things happening, feeling that dark spirit in my home again. I was waiting on Jhordyn to get home, so we could leave for a trip to Tennessee to be with my family over the holidays. I was upstairs, in my room, packing up my last things to take with me when I heard the garage door go up. After which, I immediately heard the door chimes sound as they always do when someone enters the house. I remember feeling glad that she had made it home a little earlier than anticipated, so we could go ahead and get on the road. I called out for her, but there was no answer. I called out her name, once more, as I proceeded down the stairs to her. Again, there was no answer. I opened the garage door, and her car was nowhere in sight. She was not there.

I knew at that time what it was, and I began to speak with authority against any demonic spirit. "Satan, I come against you and any plan you have devised for me! Let me remind you who I am. I'm a child of The Most High! I am the righteousness of God through Jesus Christ. You *must* not know who you're messing with!" You have absolutely NO authority over or in my home and you are no longer welcome here. Effective immediately, I am serving you your eviction notice. I cast you out through the authority given to me by The Holy Spirit!" I began to plead the blood of Jesus over my home and over the lives of everyone and everything that crossed the threshold into it. I called both my children by their names and demanded that he take his nasty hands off them, immediately! I ended my declaration and conversation with "Boy, bye! You got me mixed up!"

Immediately, he left. You see, the Word of God says that at the name of Jesus, demons *must* flee. They are no match for God. He is much too powerful for them. God gives us authority over the demons—we just have to know how to use it (Luke 10:19). I was no longer fearful but strong in the Lord and in the power of His might!

Everything in my life slowly started coming back together. I can remember being in the gym one day. I was working out on the abs machine and praying to God for a supernatural manifestation of some things He knew I desired in my life. Probably more than anything else, I wanted my purpose in life to be revealed to me. I wanted it made plain so that I could fulfill it. I strongly believe that we were all created, not to serve ourselves, but others in different capacities. My biggest fear has always been that I would live my entire life never knowing why I was placed here in this great big earth…this great big world. I can remember questioning God about this very thing many times. "God, what is it you want me to do? Why am I here? What is it you would have me do with this life you've given me? Please tell me, Father!"

Just as clearly as I could hear the music playing in my ear, I heard Him say, "I need you to give me one year." I knew what I had heard but wanted to be sure I was clear, so I asked Him what he meant. I immediately heard Him say, "I need you to be intimate with no one except me for an entire year." I heard Him clearly, but I had never been alone for that length of time before. There was always someone vying for my time and attention. I wasn't sure if I could fulfill this commitment, so I began to negotiate with Him. "God, I can do six months," I said.

I heard him very clearly. "You've been doing it your way for forty-seven years…I'm only asking you for one. I need you to be intimate with only me for one year, and I will give you the desires of your heart." What I've since come to realize is that when we are operating in Christ, He changes our desires to line up with His perfect will for our lives. The fleshly things we thought we wanted seem juvenile or insignificant in comparison to what God actually wants for us. I didn't feel confident I could do this, but I told Him I would. My lack of confidence would prove to be justified as I failed God not once but twice!

As luck would have it, BJ contacted me shortly thereafter. It was the same ole verbiage—how much he missed me and wanted to make things work. I allowed myself to see him; however, I had no intentions of becoming intimate with him. I thought I was strong enough in the Lord to withstand any temptations—but I was wrong. I laid with him, and afterwards, I paid for it. You see, I had asked God to block anything in my life from materializing if it was not from Him. Later that same day, BJ told me he was having second thoughts about us being together. I felt completely betrayed and played. For the first time since we had been together, I felt I was being treated as less than the lady in his life. I was devastated. I cried for hours until I realized what was happening. It was God answering the prayer I had prayed. I had not honored my covenant with God, and He was not pleased; however, he honored my prayer enough to do what I had asked Him to do—block what wasn't from Him.

A few months later, I had my second encounter with BJ. I felt stronger then and knew I could resist the temptations of fornicating with him. I was so very wrong. This time, I shared with him that I had entered into a covenant with God and that I could not lay with him. He said he respected that as he had always shown a reverential fear and respect for God and his authority. As the evening progressed, though, and the more libations he consumed, the more aggressive he became. He knew what he wanted, and he was used to getting it. I tried to resist, but the chemistry was too strong, and I fell prey to his advances. What he would say during our encounter, though, would shake me to my bones.

While he was making love to me, he stopped and looked down at me and said, "I don't know why you would try to deny me of what's mine. Don't you know I'm the devil! I take what I want!"

I couldn't believe what I was hearing. This was so not like him. Although he was far from perfect, he possessed a strong respect and admiration for God. He truly feared Him. This terrified and paralyzed me for that moment. I made him stop and told him not to touch me. I was in total disbelief.

The next morning, I asked him if he remembered what he had said. He said, "Tisa, I can't believe what I said to you. God, please forgive me for saying that. I'm no devil, and I don't know why I would say anything like that! I really don't know what took over me."

Just then, I realized that it wasn't him speaking to me in my bed the night before, but it was Satan—in the flesh! He was speaking to me through BJ and relishing in the fact that he was able to destroy the covenant I had formed with God—not once but twice!

I felt sick to my stomach. I was overtaken with feelings of guilt and shame once again. But it was so much deeper this time than when I had sinned before. I began to weep. What was I doing? How could I betray God again? He loved me so much that out of the billions of people in this world, He took out the time to speak to *me*, personally. He wants only the best for me and of me—and I failed him again! How stupid could I possibly be? He spoke to me and told me what I needed to do, and I failed Him. But I would not fail Him again in this area—not again. I could not allow the enemy to get the glory over my God. He deserved so much better than that from me.

After this time, I would still go out on dates but refused to become emotionally involved. Although I was successful at doing so, it became painfully obvious to me that I was just wasting my time. I found fault in everyone I dated. The smallest things would turn me off—and once I was turned off, it was nearly impossible to turn me back on. I needed to stop dating all together. I needed to be with just God. This was very new to me and extremely uncomfortable. I didn't like the feeling of being alone in the physical realm. What I had to realize was that I wasn't alone at all. God was with me, and I had a very strong extension of family and friends that God had blessed me with. I began to leverage those relationships and focus on what He wanted to do with and in me.

Once I made up my mind to stop dating completely, I started the one-year covenant all over again. Men started to come out of the wood work most especially married men. There were several in a very short period of time who made advances toward me. They were very persistent, but I resisted them all. One thing I *knew* I did not want was another woman's husband. I'm territorial and selfish when it comes to the man I'm with. But even more so, I had no desire to sow those types of seed into my life. I knew that I knew that I knew, I would eventually pay for that decision. And I wanted no parts of it. I recognized these temptations as tricks of the enemy, and that knowledge gave me the power I needed to resist them all.

There were many days I did not feel as close to God as I would have liked. There were many days I simply did not feel like praying. Many days I did not study the Word. There were many days I felt like giving in and giving up. There were many days I questioned whether or not it was even worth it. I would allow myself to wonder if it was really actually the voice of God I had heard that day in the gym. But I wanted—no, I needed to feel like I had heard from God. Deep down inside, there was absolutely no doubt in my mind that I heard what I heard. There was no reason at all for me to try to convince myself otherwise-not just because things were hard and not going the way I wanted them to go. I knew what God told me that day. Now, I just had to rely on Him to give me the strength to fulfill my commitment to Him. And it was a difficult thing to do.

I was not used to being alone. I had always had a companion in my life. And I enjoyed the company of my *boo thang*. I've never been the type to settle for being with just anyone. I'm extremely selective. I can remember my mom always preaching to my sister and me the importance of being this way. She would say "Anybody can give you a wet bottom, so make sure when you choose to have sex, it really means something." Even though I knew there was greater in store for me, from time to time, I would allow myself to become completely overtaken by feelings of loneliness and despair. I would remind God that He made me, and He knows how I am. I would question why I had to go through everything I was experiencing. And one night, out of the blue, I was reminded that if anyone is in Christ, he is a new creature and that old things have passed away (2 Corinthians 5:17). This scripture eliminates our excuse of being a product of our environment. If change is what you desire for your life, it can happen with and through Christ. My crutches were now removed and it was *game on*!

What this meant to me was that as long as we remain in the will of God and in covenant with Him, we can experience the newness of life that He has for us. But when we make the conscious decision to step outside the will of God, we revert back to what we know in the fleshly realm. There is nothing easy about this walk with God. As a matter of fact, it's downright *hard*! My bishop has said on numerous occasions that "Sin is just fun!" And he is so right. It feels good—at least for the moment that you are in it. But it has a way of making you feel empty, defeated, and guilty when it's over.

There were moments in my life when I actually enjoyed *me* time. Time to be with just me. But for the most part, I was a bit of a social butterfly. I really enjoyed the company of others. I absolutely loved hanging out with my daughters; however, they were no longer babies and wanted their own space. It was a struggle for me to let them go-to relinquish control that I actually no longer had. But I knew I had to do just that. I had to give them back to God and just pray that they would remember the things they were taught about Him. This was very difficult for me to do, and still is at times. As mothers, we don't think anyone can love our children as much as we do. I had to realize that God actually loves them more. They are much safer in His arms than they could ever be in mine.

I also enjoyed the company of my friends and family; however, very little compared to the feeling of spending quality time with a companion. It was as though God was strategically arranging things in my life to happen so that I would be alone more than I was comfortable being. My relationship with BJ was over. My kids were now independently doing their own things. My best friend received a promotion and relocated to a different state. A few close friendships I had had served their purpose and came to an abrupt end. I was lonelier now than I had ever been and it was painful at times. People who *were* reaching out in attempts to spend time were of no real interest to me. I just didn't enjoy their company as I once may have. I loved love, and I was really starting to miss being in it. Since I had asked God to block anything that was not of him, I realized I would go through times that were not necessarily comfortable. I would go through days of just not feeling all together good. But I had to go through them, and I did. In fact, I still do.

Just because I am closer to God does not mean my life is perfect. In fact, my life is nowhere close to perfection; but rather, it's a work in progress. I don't always feel close to Him. Sometimes, I go longer than I should without praying, worshipping, and studying my Word. The difference now is that I recognize it when I do. If I do sin, I don't allow feelings of guilt to keep me away from God anymore. I used to sin and then run and hide my face from Him. Now I run to Him faster than ever. I recognize the sin, and I'm quick to repent and try hard not to repeat it. That's progress.

Chapter 6

Picking up the Pieces

All my life, I have dealt with being judged solely because I am who I am. I've had so many females form negative opinions of me based solely on my physical attributes or what they perceived my life to be. As a young girl, I can remember being bullied, often times, for what I thought to be no reason at all. I felt like I was always going out of my way just to be liked by others. It was something I truly had to work hard at, as it just didn't seem to come naturally for me...still doesn't. My sister was always the one who everyone like and flocked to. She had that magnetic personality that I simply did not possess. I've always admired that about her.

I was always attracted to older guys back then...the studly, athletic type. I can recall being a high school freshman and dating a very handsome senior, star basketball player who resided a few towns over from me. He was so popular, handsome, well bred and in love with me. A few senior girls on my basketball team started taunting me one day after practice, because one of them was smitten with him. He only had eyes for me, though, and this obviously bothered them, immensely. They tried to jump me that particular day. And even though I knew I couldn't possibly win the fight, I refused to back down. The assistant principal and basketball coach broke up the fight and sent us all home. When my mother got home, I told her what happened and began to cry because I was tired of being picked on by them each time I entered a room. What my mother told me would change my life forever.

She was very hard and direct with me during her delivery. She very seldom showed any signs of weakness, nor did she tolerate it from us. "Tisa, the first thing you have to realize is that you're a Douglass offspring. Things like this come with the territory, so get used to it!" She went on to say, "As long as they're talking about you, you're doing something right. When they stop talking…then worry." These words put so many things in perspective for me. I stopped trying to fit in so much. If you liked me, fine. If not…oh well, your problem.

My life has been a plethora of emotions—an emotional rollercoaster. Had you asked me as a young woman if I ever thought I would experience half the things I actually have, I would've unequivocally said "No way!" But because of the decisions I've made, I've often times set myself up for total failure. I've always been a jack-of-all-trades and a-master-of-none kind of chick. One thing I did begin to master, though, was giving up. I became very successful at failing…at quitting what I had begun. If things became too tedious, I just stopped. And I was not always that way. I was once a real go getter who never quit a task until it was completed. This, in me, had changed, and I didn't know why. That's one thing that made the writing of this book so incredibly difficult. That's hard to admit but nonetheless true.

Unfortunately, I did start to see Bishop Bronner's prophecy over my life come to fruition. The prophecy he revealed to me after my dad passed started to take shape in me. I found myself drinking more than I should have at times. Although I never felt a dependency on alcohol, I had become way too familiar with it. I also became a bit reckless with my finances. I had always been pretty good with money; however, I started noticing that they were taking control over me instead of me controlling them. Both these flaws had been demons that my father dealt with at some points in his life. Generational curses started to show up in my life, but I was quick to recognize them. And I knew how to call on the name of Jesus to break those strongholds.

I can say that I have truly learned a lot about myself while writing this book. Prior to I'd never considered myself to be a selfish person—in part because I have a huge heart and have always been a big giver. As I wrote the various chapters of my memoirs, I realized that I have been quite selfish over the years—emotionally selfish. I've made many decisions based on what made me happy at the time not fully considering how my actions would ultimately affect others. For this, I am truly convicted. Please know that if you are one of those who have been hurt in any way because of my actions, I truly apologize. And I hope and pray you will find it in your heart to forgive me.

My life experiences have taught me how important it is to always treat people right—even when it hurts. I try to always be mindful of not passing judgment on others. I mean, when you think about it, what right do I actually have to judge anyone? What right do any of us have to do so? Think about that. If we would simply take the time to pray for others instead of ridiculing them for sinning differently than we do, how much better would this world be? I realized that I had to simply allow God to do his job—He's so good at it. Who are we to say that our sins are small and others' sins are huge? In His eyesight—it's all just sin! And wait for it—we *all* fall short! If you get nothing else from this book, *get that*!

Although it can be hard to do at times, I had to stop beating people down because I didn't understand or agree with the decisions they make. It does not serve the Body of Christ well to do so. And ask yourself how it actually benefits you. If judging others for their indiscretions actually makes you feel better about yourself, then certainly, you have work to do. It's time to point your finger inward and really allow God to do a work in you—His perfect work. I'm a fixer and have a natural tendency to want to fix everything and everyone. I've learned to simply allow people to be who they are. I realized the one thing I'll never be able to fix is another person. So I continually work on fixing myself. And I make the decision to accept or leave a person just as I found them.

For me, each day still presents its challenges. I'm just more aware now. One of my struggles has always been in how I have responded to negativity towards me or anyone I loved. In this way, I'm a lot like my mother and many of her siblings. Don't start none, won't be none! Or as my mom often said, "Don't start no SH won't be no IT!"

I've never handled that well nor have my responses always been godly; however, I've learned from many of those poor decisions. This, more than anything, still remains a struggle for me; however, I really try to think of the best response possible prior to addressing it—and I pray! What I have found through doing this is that most times, a response isn't even needed. So I bridle my tongue.

In a perfect world, everyone would get along and never do or say hurtful things to or about another. Unfortunately, the fact of the matter is that we don't live in a perfect world—not even close. I had to learn that I will never be able to control everything that is said or done against me. A wise man strategically picks his battles. I've learned to turn it over to God and allow Him to fight them for me—He's a mighty warrior! "'Vengeance is mine,' saith the Lord" (Romans 12:19). He will repay every transgression against you if you simply allow Him to do so. And make no mistake about it—He doesn't need your help.

At times, I find it difficult to resist the temptation of falling back into the same gutter He delivered me from. I have often asked God, "Am I the worst example of a Christian you've ever witnessed?" He will gently allow something to happen to let me know that I certainly am not. For instance, as I struggled to complete this book—and it certainly was a struggle—He gave me confirmation that I could do this and that I was supposed to. That confirmation, on a day I was feeling a little low, came through a conversation I had with a very close girlfriend.

At times, I listened to Satan as he tried to convince me not to complete this book. He would speak things into my spirit like "Who in the world do you think would want to read anything you have to say?" or he would say "This book is just for you, so it doesn't matter whether you finish it or not. It was designed to provide therapy for you, not to be shared with the world. Do you have any idea how people are going to view you after they read this?"

I listened at times and would go weeks even months without writing; however, when I received a nudging from the Holy Spirit, I had no choice in the matter. I had to write! I couldn't control the content even though I desperately tried because He was in total control.

One day, as I sat on my back porch, sipping on a glass of wine, attempting to do anything but write. I was moved to call my close friend, Dr. Ramona Coleman-Bell. I was almost finished but found every excuse not to complete this very last chapter. What she said to me went against every negative thought that Satan attempted to place in my mind. She told me that she had just dreamt about me the night before. I asked her what the dream was about, and she said she couldn't remember it all; but she could recall that I was sharing something important with her. When she revealed this to me, I told her about the book that I was writing. This is important because I had not revealed this to many people at all—not even those closest to me.

I shared with her that I was hesitant to do so for fear that I would not finish it or that it would be a total failure. Who was I to think I had anything meaningful to share with the world? Her words after that shook me and gave me the strength I needed to get off my tail and complete this literary piece of work.

She said, "Tisa, I'm so proud of you. It takes a great deal of courage to do what you're doing. You always have a way of seeing the very best in people. You've been blessed with the gift of making others feel good about themselves. I don't care if they're ugly, fat, or anything else—you can find a way to make them feel good about who they are."

This brought tears to my eyes. I could barely finish our conversation because of how hard I was crying. Allow me to explain why. You see, she is the friend who painted me the perfect portrait of what *true* friendship looked like. She chose to love me when anyone else would have and possibly *should* have written me off for good. She decided to love me through my transgression against her. She was my friend who was in love with my husband when I decided I wanted him for myself. I'm not sure I could have been as big a person as she was. In fact, I know I couldn't have been. Her heart was so pure, and her love so strong for me until I didn't understand it—'til now.

You see, that was the love of God in her. He loves us unconditionally. His love for us never ends. It conquers all things, and it never fails. I was so undeserving of the love she displayed to me after that point just as we are all so undeserving of Christ's love for us. She taught me unconditional friendship, and I thank God that regardless of the many miles between us, we are as close now as we have ever been. What a mighty God we serve!

I can remember how easy it was for me to hold on to anger... to keep bitterness and unforgiveness in my heart. But when I truly realized that forgiveness really was for me and not the other person, it became impossible for me to remain that way. Many times, we want to punish others for offending us. I really think that's a natural feeling, initially; however, you can not hold on to it. There is no way in the world you can have inner peace and unforgiveness dwelling within the same body. I chose to have inner peace. The day I let it all go, I felt as though a ton of bricks had been lifted from me. I felt so free, and it felt so good! I asked God to take it all away from me. "God, this is too much for me to carry and I just don't want it anymore. Please remove this from me, so I can experience your perfect peace."

The choice we make to forgive others truly serves us well. When we refuse to forgive others, we make it harder on ourselves. The offenders are going about their lives with no concern of us or our feelings, while our insides are in knots thinking about how they did us. Do yourselves a favor and let it go. Trust that God's got you and he will repay the debt owed you.

I want to encourage you all to just love somebody—everybody! When you truly have a heart full of love, there is no room for anything else to enter in. There are many I have parted ways with in the past. Some friends are but for a season. However, I wish them all well and harbor no ill will toward them anymore. I'm free from that bondage. I can boldly declare that I am no longer saved by association (because Momma 'nem were), but I now have my own very personal relationship with the Savior. And I wouldn't trade it for anything in the world!

There is something I need you all to realize. It will be tough for many to get. It will be a huge pill for some to swallow. It will offend many who consider themselves set apart. But the fact of the matter is that it's the truth. When you operate in the truth, there is a freedom that comes along with it. (John 8:32) Are you ready for it? Really ready? Ok, good. Here it goes. WE ALL SIN!

Like it or not, it remains true now and forever. There are none who are without sin. (Romans 3:23) Yes I said it. Yes that includes you as well. Whether you're fornicating, lying, cheating, stealing, hurting others, gossiping about others, standing in judgement of others, murdering, or anything else that is not like God and His perfect heart for us, it's sin. There are no big sins and little sins. It's ALL sin.

I had to realize that I will never be perfect. I will always have character flaws. I will always struggle with one thing or the other. But the great news is that God still loves me. He will never cease in caring for us...each and every one. When I realized this, it freed me. I will and *should* always strive to do good; however, I no longer place unrealistic expectations on myself. Expectations which are impossible for me to achieve-*Perfection*. The only result I can expect to get when I set expectations for myself that I can never achieve is disappointment. I choose not to live my life in constant disappointment of myself and neither should you. Life is meant to be good...really good. That's what I choose. That's what I have.

Fortunately, His goodness is not only for me. You can make a choice to have it as well. With Christ, all things are possible. Trust Him. He's got you!

I hope this book has blessed you all in some way—this is my sincere prayer. And I would like to offer Christ to anyone reading this who does not know Him for yourself. All it takes to be saved is to confess with your mouth that Jesus is Lord over your life. All you have to do is welcome Him in. He's patiently waiting for you. If He is not Lord of your life but you desire Him to be, please just speak this short prayer:

Jesus, I believe that you are Lord of my life. I believe you died on the cross to cover my sins. Please, God, forgive me of my transgressions against you and cleanse me right now. I welcome you into my heart today, and I believe I am a new creature because you now live in me! Amen

If you sincerely said that prayer, I believe you are now a part of God's wonderful family. I am so happy that you made the decision to join us. Your life will never be the same.

Welcome home, my friends. Peace and abundant blessings be unto you!

About the Author

Tisa Batey received her undergrad Bachelor of Science Degree in Mass Communication with an emphasis in journalism from Austin Peay State University in Clarksville, Tennessee. She was able to express herself through her writing shortly thereafter while she served as lead news anchor and reporter at a small network in Roane County, Tennessee. Although she had a passion for writing, she decided to change career paths in the mid-'90s and left to pursue a career in business management.

Although she has had a successful career, she considers Motherhood to be her greatest accomplishment. Her two beautiful daughters are her WHY! Family is very important to her. As a result, she is deeply rooted in many of the old-fashioned traditions and values instilled in her as a child. The author is also a very proud member of the illustrious Alpha Kappa Alpha Sorority, Inc.

She accepted Christ as her personal Lord and Savior at a very young age, but her life has been anything but spotless. Her love for God did not stop her from making poor decisions or from sinning, but she is so grateful that His love for her never ceased through it all. She has learned that being a Christian and having your own personal relationship with God does not make you perfect—it simply makes you aware.

CPSIA information can be obtained
at www.ICGtesting.com
Printed in the USA
LVHW051158190919
631578LV00010B/218